**Immortal Investments Publishing**

# 22 Yellow Roses

*To Brittany*
*Good Health*
*Good Luck !*

*Owen Bud Hucul*

# By Clarence "Bud" Hucul

**Immortal Investments Publishing**

# 22 Yellow Roses

*"Give a girl a bat, a ball, and a place to play*

*and she'll never go astray!"* - Clarence Hucul

# By Clarence "Bud" Hucul

Published by
Immortal Investments Publishing
www. immortalinvestmentspublishing.com
35122 W. Michigan Avenue, Wayne, Michigan 48184
800-475-2066


Publisher's Cataloging-In-Publication Data
( Prepared by The Donohue Group, Inc. )

Hucul, Clarence.
  22 yellow roses / by Clarence Hucul.

    p. ;  cm.

    ISBN: 0-9723637-9-3
1. Hucul, Clarence. 2. Coaches (Athletics)--Michigan--Biography. 3.
All Sports (Softball team) 4. Softball for women--Michigan. 5.
Softball teams--Michigan. 6. Softball--Coaching. I. Title. II. Title:
Twenty-two yellow roses

GV881.3 .H83 2006
796.357/8/092

# ACKNOWLEDGEMENTS

I want to thank Diane for allowing me my privacy to write this story.

I could not have proceeded without the help of Bonnie, who typed, proofread and edited the manuscript.

I also want to thank Pat for his input.

Thank you to Immortal Investments Publishing for making this dream a reality. To the Publisher Michael Reddy a big thank you for all of your time and assistance in seeing this project come to fruition. To Jennifer Moitozo for her hard work and dedication, Thank you. Also, to Barb Guniea at Sans Serif, Inc.thank you for creating such a great dust jacket.

# Dedication

The young women whose softball team I was privileged to coach inspired me to tell this story, which is dedicated to them.

# INTRODUCTION

*"Give a girl a bat, a ball, and a place to play and she'll never go astray."- Clarence Hucul*

The story you are about to read is about a group of girls who didn't have the best grades or softball skills. Some were poor and low in social status.

If you know a young girl in her teens, you also know that these girls faced choices that would affect their life and their future. Sometimes you may share their experiences and feel their pain. Other times you may see their vision, blocked by inequality and injustice. In the end, you will see that a young girl doesn't need to drive a car or have a credit card to be a somebody.

# <u>22 YELLOW ROSES</u>
A story based on actual events

It was a cool November day in Madison Heights, Michigan. We had recently buried my father. Now, both parents were taken from me through heart failure.

I was pondering on what to do with my life. I had spent a couple of years playing pro baseball and did some scouting work for a Major League baseball club. I liked sports, so with the little bit of money my dad left to me, I opened a small sport shop. I called it THE SPORT SHOP - ALL SPORTS. We dealt mostly in team uniforms. I couldn't afford to pay for any help, so there I was – a one-man operation.

It was hard, being tied down to the store eight to eleven hours a day, having to call out for food. Before long, sales people came by the dozen, selling me this and telling me I can't get along without that product. Little by little, coaches and teams started placing orders for uniforms, bats, baseballs and gloves and everything else their sponsors were willing to pay for.

Sometimes after work I would go out to watch some of the teams that were wearing my uniforms. This took a lot of my time and it became annoying to my wife. Balancing my home life, work, and my love for baseball was a constant challenge.

A second springtime came, and the team orders started coming in. Business was good and the bills were getting paid on time. There were many late nights when I would stuff baseball jerseys in boxes for UPS pick-up in the morning, to be sent to the shop to be lettered.

One afternoon, some girls came in to order t-shirts with numbers on the backs. They brought in an envelope with their teammates' names and the amount of money collected from each. They said they had no sponsor, so they could only afford to get t-shirts. They were quite upset at the fact that most businesses just sponsor men's teams. Some of their teammates worked after school to earn money; and the rest of the team was out of school and worked other jobs.

I took their money and placed the order. A few of the girls came back about two weeks later and said that they needed their softball t-shirts, but they couldn't pay the balance of money on the order, because they had to pay their team entry fee to play in the league. They also said that the league wouldn't let them play their first game unless they had softball jersey with numbers on their backs. I believed the girls, because they were sincere and embarrassed. So, I said, "Take the t-shirts and pay the balance when you can." Off they went, happy and determined to play in the league.

From time to time, the girls came into the store to pay on their account. They said the team wasn't doing well; they were losing games, and even their boyfriends were laughing from the stands. The boyfriend of one of the players was coaching them, but he was barred from the league for drinking beer and being intoxicated in the coach's box. Some would think this was funny, but these girls were serious about wanting to play the game of softball.

A couple more weeks passed and the girls came in again. This time they paid their account in full. They told me that they had to forfeit the last game because only eight players showed up. Three players quit because they weren't playing enough and one player's boyfriend kept her away because of the arguing and people laughing at them. I told the three players who were in the store that day to tell their teammates to stop by the store the day before their next game. Puzzled as they were, they agreed.

In the next couple of days, I hustled to get 14 individual travel bags, used to store the players' gloves, shoes, and hats. A couple of days later, the girls showed up at the store, curious and anxiously wondering what was awaiting them. I put the bags and hats on the counter and said, "They're yours free, just finish out the season – don't quit. Stick together, and focus on playing softball and enjoying it."

They whole-heartedly thanked me; however, some of the pictures on my desk ignited some of the players to pursue questions about my baseball background. I told them, "I did some scouting for the St. Louis Cardinals and played a little professional baseball."

Sunday morning, I was cleaning up the store when four of the girls from the team came knocking at my door. I let them in. Sad as they seemed, I cheerfully asked, "How's the team doing? Did you win your game?" They didn't answer, and I knew what was coming next! They said, "We know you're busy and your time is valuable, but would you consider spending some time with us at a couple of practices?"

I hesitated a bit, then said, "Look – tell you what I'll do. When, where and what time is your next game? I'll stop by and watch you play." They seemed relieved and left the store, looking a little better than when they came in.

The following Tuesday, I locked up the store and made it over to their 7:00 p.m. game. I was a little late, I believe. The game had just started. They looked good in their t-shirts and hats, their carry-all bags tucked under the players' bench.

I watched them play for about three innings. A couple of players were talking to their boyfriends and friends in the stands. One player was standing by the bleachers smoking a cigarette. Another player was so busy talking to friends in the bleachers that she didn't know she was up to bat.

Defensively, they missed ground balls through their legs, couldn't judge fly balls, and threw to the wrong bases. And they even laughed at themselves when they made these blunders. I saw enough, and left. I wasn't mad. I felt sorry for them because they didn't know why they were playing so poorly. Maybe some of them thought they were supplying some kind of entertainment!

A couple of days passed and they came to the store asking me why I didn't stay for the whole game. I gave them a serious look and they didn't smile – they got the message. They said, "See, this is why we need coaching." I answered, "You need discipline first, then coaching." I expressed my opinion about visiting friends in the bleachers, smoking while playing softball, and running around the field chasing a ball when they had no idea where that ball would land.

They answered, "Anything else?" I said, "Yes, I can understand why people are laughing at you – you're not a softball team – you're an entertainment group." They were sorry they asked, but I was only telling them the truth.

They left mad!

I didn't hear from them for a couple of weeks. Then one Sunday morning while I was at the store, one of the players came in. She very politely thanked me for coming to their game and explained to me that the players talked over what I had said. They all agreed that they wanted to play softball seriously and would greatly appreciate any help I could offer them. Half the season was over and they hadn't won a game yet. They wanted to finish the season and they were tired of losing and being laughed at.

Somehow, I knew this time that they were serious and embarrassed. I knew what she was looking for me to say: "Coach us – work with us." I knew this would be no easy task. The time it would take and the hard practices would do them in. Before I could tell her it was impossible for me to coach the team, seven more players came through the door, quietly approaching, not saying anything, but looking at the one player who had been talking with me for the last hour. They were looking for any body language that would give away my decision. It was silent – no one said anything. I looked up at them and said, "Look – I'll tell you what I'll do. You bring your team here to the store Wednesday night, 8 sharp."

The next couple of days, I was busy at the store. Orders were coming in, salesmen were calling on me, and it appeared to me that some sporting goods salesmen were loading me up too heavily with merchandise that I wouldn't be able to pay for when the bills came due.

# TEAM MEETING

Wednesday evening, they came. Not the usual 10 –11 players, but 14 players showed up, looking happy and showing politeness. I locked the store door and sat them all down on the carpet. I looked at them and said, "Do you want me to be your coach, is this what this is all about?" Everyone responded, "YES!" I asked them, "How many coaches have you played for while playing softball?" Some answered, "Just our high school coach," and some didn't answer.

I paused for a moment, and said that I would not be an easy coach to play for, that I would be giving up time from my business that it could interrupt any success I may enjoy. I needed to know how much time they could devote to softball. I asked how many players were in high school and playing high school softball, and how many others had jobs or no jobs or commitments. I also asked, "Do any of you have visions of going to college? How would your parents feel about your commitment to playing organized softball, once you're ready?"

Then the question came: "What do you mean about being ready?" I paused and looked directly at them. "You can't even win games in the league you're playing in. You don't know the fundamentals of softball. You have too many distractions and you're eventually going to hurt yourselves playing the game the wrong way." Many of them responded, "So what do we do?" I answered: "You're here. This is a new beginning. From here on, I'll be your coach, but will expect full cooperation, dedication, loyalty and no second-guessing."

Their words came out: "No problem." I then said, "The first thing I'm going to do is pull you out of that league you're in. You won't learn anything playing in there, and the competition is not in your best interest."
I told them that Tuesday night at 7, we would meet again. This time the meeting would be at the field. "And bring your softball gear. I will expect you to be there if you're planning on playing on the team – no exceptions." Some asked me about playing and practicing before Tuesday's meeting. I answered adamantly, "NO!" That didn't seem to be a problem for anyone. Some said, "Thank you, Mr. Bud! We'll be there."

The next day I called the league director to inform him that the team would no longer be showing up for games and that all their games could be forfeited to their opponents. He wasn't too happy about it, but at least he was notified.

I kept busy at the store and thought about these players I was about to coach. I had four players in high school; four players working part-time, trying to earn money for college; three players of one-parent families; two players living with relatives; and one player, so I was told, abused and staying with a boyfriend.

I really was giving this decision some strong mental searching about myself and how I was going to handle all this. It seemed to me that most of the players were in search of a  purpose. They were eager and I sincerely admired that. I also knew that their athletic ability needed discipline, work and strength. I believed they displayed the motivation to learn.

# MEETING ON THE BALL FIELD

I showed up ten minutes early for Tuesday night's meeting. To my surprise, 19 players showed up. I thanked them for coming and asked them to sit down and relax; this meeting could be long. I told them my name was "Coach Bud" – not, Old Fart or Mr. Drill Sergeant.

"We will respect each other. I am not here to win a popularity contest; in fact, some of you will probably hate me in due time. Forget about who coached you before, or told you how to play softball. You're going to learn to play softball the right way. Practices will be long and they will intensify. Compliments will be few. Tears will come! And eventually tears will be replaced with wins. There will be no games for a while, just practices and more practices. I will need your dedication and loyalty and you will also give this to one another. Some of you will not play at times. I don't expect you to sit on the bench and pout. Show an interest in and enthusiasm for your teammates who are playing. And when it's your turn to play, you will be shown the same. Those of you who are going to high school – keep good grades. It could open a door for you later. Don't talk behind your teammates' backs. In the end, I promise you no one will ever again laugh at you playing softball while you're a member of this team. When the season ends, if you haven't learned anything or haven't improved your game, then I will stand up and you can tell me anything you want. Now – if you have any questions, please direct them now."

No one said a word.

I said, "There's no light on this diamond, so we won't be practicing tonight." I instructed two players who lived in a nearby city to contact their city Recreation Department and start securing practice permits for fields four days a week. "I want the practices to be away from your distractions and friends. Everyone fill out these forms with your name, address, phone number, and birth date. I'll call you soon for your first practice. Your friends and other players may quiz you about why you dropped out of the league. They will eventually know you're practicing softball. Try to play this low-key. I want to practice without distractions."

# FIRST PRACTICE

We secured a field seldom used because it was small in size and had very little parking. This would be ideal.

When I asked the players to gather around for a short meeting, I suddenly realized we now had 22 players. I welcomed the new faces and suggested that the regulars please fill them in with what happened at our last meeting so they would know what to expect. They answered, "We did – that's why they're here."

I told two of the regular players to go to my car. In the back seat were a couple of boxes. "Bring the boxes back here to the field." When they returned, I handed out sweatshirts, t-shirts, shorts, hats and socks. I told them, "These are your practice outfits. Wear them clean to practices." The colors were rust with tan and white lettering, spelling out ALL SPORTS. That was the name of my sport shop and these were going to be our team colors.

I first picked up a softball and explained how to grip the ball across the seams, "So that when you release your throw, you will have four seams rotating for better velocity." I demonstrated how to swing the bat. "You actually are throwing the bat at the ball, and while doing this your wrists turn over with the swing." I took them through the base paths and explained to them, "When running the bases, touch the inside corner of the base with your left foot."

We went through offensive and defensive techniques. I explained to them that, "Before you start your practice, stretch out your muscles" and appointed a couple of players who did this in high school to lead them through these stretching exercises. I reminded them that stretching out before and after practice would help prevent injury and sore muscles.

We spent much of the first two weeks fielding grounders and fly balls, running bases, and learning to swing bats properly. There was no batting practice during the first two weeks.

After about 13 practices of throwing, catching, running and skill sessions, we started on batting practice. We started out with eight hits and running to first base on the eighth hit. They would stay on first base and run to second base on the second hit of the next batter.

Once the practice workouts and team meetings were a regular routine, we all began to share a common vision to play the game of softball right and enjoy the season, letting the results play out. About two months had passed. The team was learning well and I thought they enjoyed the sessions.

I had been closing the store earlier for softball practices. It began to lack the full attention it needed; bills were being paid slowly and mostly late. Between the store and the time demanded by the team, it was dragging me down, but I never wanted my team to observe this in me.

The team was getting antsy to play some kind of competitive game, so I organized an intra-squad game between them. We called it the tan and white game. When they made a mistake, I would stop the game and explain the situation. I was able to see the results of our practices after about four intra- squad games. Some players were short on confidence in themselves and some were hesitating on hard-hit ground balls, so one by one, I lined them up in front of home plate. I stood by the pitcher's mound and hit grounders extra hard at their feet. Over time, they got the message.

I assigned two players to the softball equipment, one player to the First Aid Kit, and two players to the water detail. In case I was late, they had the routine down pat to start the practice. I informed them that immediately after every practice or game, there would always be a team meeting on the field to discuss the practice or game.

It was now the middle of August, and some of the better teams were preparing for nationals. Their regular season games were over, and these teams were always looking for scrimmage games before they left for nationals. So, I decided to call a coach in Ohio I had known for a while. We agreed on a double-header in Ohio.

# FIRST EXHIBITION GAME

We discussed the trip to Ohio and what to expect. I told them, "I don't care if we win or lose. Just do the things we worked on."

We organized five cars. I gave them gas money and made reservations at a motel in the town where we were playing our games. We lost both games, 7-3 and 6-1. We played a good team and we didn't get blown out. Before we cleared out of the motel, we had a team meeting. I told them I saw some good things and I saw some not-so good things. I told them we would go over all this back home at our own field. I paid the motel bill and we left.

The following weekend, I worked in the store, checking my mail and cleaning it up. Delinquent notices were coming in on merchandise I'd ordered for the store. I started ordering from different companies that would ship on credit. I didn't know it at the time, but this would prove to be a very costly mistake for me.

Curious parents and other players started showing up at our practices. Most parents were offering to help. Some were complaining about their daughters spending too much time on softball. All this was something I'd expected. We were getting the reputation of being a snooty bunch, isolated from other local teams. Some of my players lost some friends, but most of them gained loyal fans and respect for themselves and others.

I decided to schedule a game with one of the teams from the league that I had pulled the team out of earlier in the year. The game was all set. We even had real umpires. We had a good crowd. During the game, our girls were hitting the ball much too hard - the other team was shying away from the hard-hit balls. We were running too fast on the bases, confusing the other team about what base they were throwing the ball to. The game got out of hand – we were winning 14-1. Eventually, we started making some mistakes; the other team had set the tempo of the game as a comedy of errors. Finally, when the game ended we had won, 22-3. The players were laughing and happy.

As usual, after the game we went into the outfield for our team meeting. I looked at them and said, "You started out great! Then you got sloppy, because they played sloppy. You thought you won the game in the third inning, so you relaxed, and got a little lazy and careless. Remember, you came from this league. People laughed at the way you played. Don't anyone plan on leaving. We are staying and practicing." They took five rounds of six hits and ran the bases three times. Two hours later we had another meeting. I said, "This will not happen again." I gave them the next practice day off and scheduled a team meeting at the store in four days.

I needed time in the store. Things were closing in on me. Creditors were calling; merchandise was being shipped COD. My bank account was low. I can't blame the team for this. They had been loyal and done everything I asked them to do. I never saw a bunch of girls work so hard at softball and believe in the system of winning that they were starting to feel.

The team meeting at the store arrived, and I informed the team that we were going to Covington, Kentucky, for a tournament the next week. I also had a surprise for them: two sets of new uniforms for the tournament, new travel bags to match, and new jackets. I said, "You earned it. I'm proud of you." I also thanked them for their hard work and loyalty. I told them I thought they were ready for some real competition.

We had two practices before we started the five-hour drive to Covington. I gave them a rooming list and gas allowance, and we discussed the rules for our stay at the motel: no drinking, no guys, no parties, and 10:00 p.m. curfew, unless we were playing.

# OUR FIRST TOURNAMENT

We arrived at the motel in Cincinnati, Ohio, which is just across the river from Covington. Our first game was rain delayed, so we took batting practice in the motel parking lot. After about three hours we were finally called to play. We beat a team from Winchester, Indiana, 5-3 and trounced an Akron, Ohio, team 10-1. We then lost to a Louisville, Kentucky, team, 6-4. That put us in the losers' bracket, and when you get into the losers' bracket with 27 teams, you can expect to play 4-5 games a day. Sunday morning came. There were 12 teams left. We won 8-3 over a London, Kentucky, team. We had a two-hour break. Then we played a team from Cleveland, Ohio, to eleven innings and won 6-5. We handed a team from Jellico, Tennessee, a 4-0 loss. We now had a three-hour break. It was down to four teams remaining in the tournament. Our next game was at 9 p.m. We lost 4-1 to a team from Lexington, Kentucky. We were tired. And this was their first tournament of real competition. I was proud of them. We packed up the 3rd Place Trophy and headed back to Michigan. It was a happy ride and they somehow knew that this might be the season finale. I told them there would be a team meeting at the store on Tuesday night.

At the store on Monday, I spent time answering creditors' calls and thinking about the season and the sport shop, contemplating my next move.

Tuesday night's meeting came. Everyone showed up, bringing their uniforms all cleaned, but somehow they weren't happy. They had just finished 3$^{rd}$ in a 27-team tournament with competition from some of the best teams. I told them that I had talked to a college coach who coached one of the teams in the tournament. She informed me that she had been impressed with our young team, their familiarity with the true fundamentals of softball, and their aggressive desire to win. Most of all, she admired the discipline we displayed while playing.

I said, "Some of you will be starting back to school shortly and will probably be playing basketball and volleyball." I expressed my opinion that, "Some of you could be college material for a softball scholarship. But this challenge will not be easy. College softball coaches don't have the budget to recruit, like the guys' baseball coaches. It also will mean staying in shape and softball-sharp, which means you'll have to continue to practice softball. Some coaches will expect videos of your playing ability. Once on the college campus, you can work out for the coach. Besides, an in-person visit to a college gives you a feel for the atmosphere and an idea of what to expect."

Some of my players who weren't college material were worried that they would be excluded from practicing and being a part of all this. I told them that my intention was to keep the team intact, working out through the fall and bad weather. I told them to "put your uniforms back in your duffle bags. The ALL SPORTS Express continues."

The next few days I was getting feedback from parents who couldn't afford sending them to colleges for tryouts. The team wanted to keep going together, but I had this dilemma – no funds, no time. My sport shop was in serious jeopardy.

I had a great loyal bunch of girls wanting to support the better players in securing a college softball scholarship. I had some players whose parents didn't have the funds and some parents who just didn't care. I also had some players whose grades weren't that good.

I stressed to all the players, "In school, focus on your grades and prepare yourself for your ACT tests. The ACT scores may be a good goal to enter college, but it should not be the only measure to judge a student athlete to become a successful person. Some players have disabilities in learning, and are a little short on the grades."

My game plan was to keep the interest high with practicing in order to keep the season going. I started contacting some college coaches for the girls who were seniors and the ones with the ability to pursue this goal. I was also getting feedback from some of the girls' high school coaches – that their chances were slim and none, and that I was misleading them.

Finally, I called a meeting at the store. The players and whatever parents wanted to participate were welcome. I started the meeting by telling everyone how hard this team had worked and that everyone should be proud of them. I also informed them that some of these players deserved to further their education by pursuing a softball scholarship. "Some may succeed and some may not. They deserve the chance – they earned it."

I answered their questions concerning some of their high school coaches. I told them that there were some good high school coaches, but there were also some lazy ones. High school softball season in Michigan is short because of the weather. Most high school coaches are underpaid and won't take the time to contact a college. Most of them don't even know how to expose their players to a college coach. I saw some of their coaching results in the players we played against. I had a message to deliver and I delivered it!! We had a good meeting.

We kept practicing as the weather was getting colder. Everyone wanted money. Between the softball team expenses and my own, I was feeling doomed for bankruptcy. I started to order from even more new vendors on credit, using the sale of new merchandise to pay for some of the old bills. Thanksgiving was approaching; the weather was turning cold. We kept playing softball. I did most of the pitching and it was taking a toll on me. I was getting hit by batters in the ankles, hip and legs. We did mostly batting and running. It was too cold for them to do much throwing.

# OUR FIRST FLORIDA TRIP

I called another team meeting at the store. I informed five of the players that I had contacted some college coaches in Florida. I knew that school was out for the holidays during Christmas, so I told them we could visit three colleges during the Christmas holidays. We needed two cars to travel. I was going to supply the gasoline and motel expenses – they just needed to bring food money. Most of the other players insisted on going, too, so the whole team was to work out in Florida. It would be good for the team to get away. Some of the other players would experience colleges and could watch the tryouts. We now had four cars, and I asked a good friend to assist me in coaching. I really needed the help. We discussed all the travel rules and departed for Florida the day after Christmas.

After 22 hours of driving, we arrived in Tampa. I told the players to get some sleep, and we would meet in seven hours in a motel meeting room. The meeting was short. I told the players who were trying out for the college coach to remember to stretch out before and after the workout. I told them not to wear clothing with any college logos on them. I also told them to try to relax and have some fun. "Keep your heads up – even if you miss a ground ball. Don't mentally or physically quit out there." I also told the players who weren't trying out to sit in the stands but not to cheer or yell out anything during the workouts. I told them there would be a 10 p.m. curfew that night and that I was going over to the college to go over the workout times with the college coach.

On my way back to the motel, I noticed that one of my players was by a party store talking to some people. As I approached the store, I observed her drinking, and it wasn't soda pop! She froze as I got out of my car. I told her to get into the car. We drove back to the motel, which was about five blocks away. I told her to remain in her room. I asked one of her roommates to get her some supper in her room – she was grounded. Even though this was not one of the girls trying out at the college, she was still a team member.

I went to my room and called the airlines. There was a 10:20 p.m. flight back to Detroit that night. I called the girl's mother and informed her that her daughter had violated a team rule of behavior. I also told her mother that I had made a reservation for her daughter on Delta Airlines, and that she needed to call and prepay the airline ticket – that I was taking her to Tampa airport for the flight. The last thing I said was that her daughter would tell the rest of the story to her.

When I took the player to the airport, I told her roommates that there was a problem and that she was going home that night. The situation was not to be discussed anymore on this trip. I didn't want the players trying out for the college team to be distracted by this. Everyone was cooperative and the group was quiet. The players were told about an 8 a.m. wake up. We had to be at the college field at 10 a.m.

I took the suspended player to the airport. There were not many words exchanged.

# OUR FIRST COLLEGE VISIT

Morning came. I could tell that the tryout players were nervous – no appetite for breakfast, forgetting some of their softball gear. We got it all together and arrived at the college softball field at 9:30 a.m. The players were going through their stretch exercises and warming up. The college coach came. I introduced my players, complimented her on the condition of the softball field, and said, "They're all yours!"

The coach had the players take batting practice and timed them running to first base. Two of my players were infielders and the other two players were outfielders. They fielded ground balls and fly balls. She tested their arms for strength and accuracy. She knew what she was doing. After the workout, the coach offered a tour of the campus with a couple of her own college players.

The rest of my players and I just stayed out of the way and went off by ourselves. After about an hour and a half, the players returned from their campus visit. They seemed pleased, and they told me the coach had taken their names and addresses, etc. One of the college players walked over and told me that her coach wanted to talk to me.

I went to the coach's office and we talked about two of our team members - both of my infielders. We discussed Pell Grant money, and she let me know that her budget was tight. She said that she might try to put a package together for one player for sure. She liked them both. She asked about their grades and family life. She said that she wasn't going to make any decisions before "Letter of Intent" time, which was about the first of March, and that she would be in touch. I didn't want to push anything further. I thanked her for the invite, complimented the campus, and wished her luck in her coming season.

The players and I went out to lunch and discussed the player who had been suspended for drinking and sent home to Detroit. I let them do what they wanted for the rest of the day.

The next morning we started back north with a stop in Gainesville, Florida, for another workout with a college coach. I thought the workouts in Gainesville were even better than in Tampa. The college coach was impressed, but it was too soon to expect any indication of a future commitment. We spent two days in Gainesville before heading back to Michigan. We all were tired, driving straight through to Detroit.

I needed time at the store to figure out what I was doing. The team expenses: equipment, uniforms and college travel were mounting up to thousands of dollars. I was really getting myself in deeper and deeper.

It wasn't much of a Christmas or New Year's for my personal life. My wife was showing signs of having enough of all of this. "I haven't been much of a husband the past seven months," I apologized, but it didn't seem to offer any answers. I explained to my wife that this girls' softball team and I had formed a bond and that I was hoping some good could become of it – even, perhaps, getting a few girls into college who couldn't afford it, with a softball scholarship. My wife asked where she fit into all of these plans. I think she knew the answer, but she wanted me to say it. I couldn't tell her anything – I didn't know what to say that would make up for my lack of time with her. We had been married 16 years. It wasn't fair to her, I know – I was sorry. She had made all the house payments lately and paid all the household bills. She knew the store was coming apart and our marriage was heading in the same direction.

I spent the next few late nights at the store, buried deep in the bills and the softball team. All of this, along with my home life, was aggravating me to not sympathize with my merchandise vendors' bills. Some of these salesmen had oversold me, but down deep, I knew I had simply neglected the business and my wife. I honestly could not get out of this financial mess with my store. I was robbing Peter to pay Paul. I couldn't weigh the successful softball team and some of the players securing softball scholarships with the business mess I was in.

We had planned an Easter vacation trip to a college in West Virginia. This trip involved the whole team. We were playing the college in a scrimmage game, my girls against a Division I college team. I was proud, but this trip would cost about $1,500.00. Here we go again – no money. I was milking the store money and I wasn't paying the bills.

I also had scheduled trips to Evanston, Illinois; Iowa City, Iowa; and Omaha, Nebraska. This involved five key players on our team. My plan was that scheduling all these campus visits and tryouts would strengthen my players and document what colleges were interested in them and where they had been. College coaches were asking me who else was interested in my players and where they had been, in reference to college campuses. The more college coaches my players talked to and the more colleges they visited, they appeared more credible – and it was working!

My team and I kept in contact with our team meetings twice a month. Easter vacation was approaching. Five of my players were playing high school softball, so their coaches had them working out in the gym. When the second week of March came, these players were working out outdoors with their high school team. A couple of high school coaches didn't like the idea of sharing these players with me on some weekends for our own practices. I could see the stress and I was tired of people confusing these girls about their softball commitments. I told my players that if they were playing on their high school team, I wouldn't expect them to play in our league games until their high school season was over; however, I would expect them to show up once in a while for our meetings and practices, in order to stay focused a little on what we were doing – especially the players trying out for colleges. I got the idea that some of the high school coaches and their players were either jealous or selfish about the success of our team and all the college interest that was now surfacing in some of our players. The college coaches were talking to me, not the high school coaches. Maybe this was part of the problem. Maybe this problem woke up some of these high school coaches.

About a week prior to Easter vacation, two of my players came to my store with a serious problem. One of my key college recruit players was pregnant. She could not talk to her mother, and she was scared. Only the two players and I knew about this. I told the two players to bring her to the store so we could all have a discussion, if that's what she wanted. So, the next night the three players showed up at the store. I tried to offer a relaxed atmosphere. We all sat down. The pregnant player said, "Well, I guess you know my situation." I answered, "Yes," and said, "What do you want to do?" She said, "There is no way my parents can find out, or any of the kids at school." I said, "That's going to be up to you all not to discuss the situation with anyone." She said that she had thought all of this through and this was her decision and terminated the pregnancy.

# WEST VIRGINIA TRIP

Two days prior to Good Friday, we had a team meeting at the store to discuss the West Virginia trip to play the college in a double-header. The five players who were playing high school softball had already played two games for their high school team. Only one high school scheduled a practice for a Saturday prior to Easter Sunday, so my one player told her high school coach that she was going out of town and wouldn't be at practice.

Late Friday afternoon we all left for West Virginia. We would spend Friday night at the motel resting for the Saturday double-header. I told my players, "Don't think about playing a college team. It's just another ball game. Remember all the things we worked on and focus on the games."

Our players looked sharp! They did all the right things. They were fired up! We won both games, 2-0 and 3-1. Even though the college coach said she was missing three starters – they were out of town on Easter break – she was nice and complimented our team. The whole team had a campus visit. This was a good experience for them.

Easter morning we all had breakfast together at the motel. We then started back to Michigan.

The players were still on Easter break, so we practiced three times. I had to get the team ready for our leagues. I had entered our team in two leagues and we were starting league play in six days, minus the five high school players. These five players were starters on our team, so we had to prepare to go ahead and start the season without them. We still had 13 good players to start the season and I felt confident.

The five players represented four different high schools. One of the high school coaches was very understanding and even thanked me for the improvement in the player on his high school squad. Of course, she was my starting third baseperson. I went out to see her first two games with the high school team. I was very supportive of all five players playing high school softball. I only wished all the other high school coaches had been as supportive of the total situation, had let the girls play softball and let them continue having visions and aspirations of furthering their education through a softball scholarship.

We won our first game in one of the leagues and would begin play in the other league the next week.

The store situation was not improving. We were selling baseball and softball uniforms, but I had trouble getting delivery because of slow paying and bad credit. I didn't want to close the store and walk away; failure was not on my agenda. I kept stalling the creditors and paid some of the CODs with customers' deposits for uniform orders.

# SUSPENSION

It was early Friday morning. I received a call from the parent of one of my players. The parent wanted to meet with me; he said it was very important. He came to my shop. He said that the high school girls' softball coach had suspended his daughter from the team because she played for our All Sports team in the games against the college team in West Virginia. The high school coach told his daughter that it was against high school rules to play in an organized softball game while she was playing high school softball. I looked at the girl's dad and said, "Unbelievable! Why are these coaches putting their players through political maneuvers and the disillusionment of erasing their aspirations for bettering themselves with a college scholarship?" We talked for about an hour and agreed that we should seek some legal advice. Here we had a girl playing softball on her high school team and also playing for our team, extending her time and sweat to improve her ability to become a better player. And, we had some high school coaches who didn't take the time to go out of the bounds of their programs and beyond their immediate responsibilities to lend any extra assistance to expose their players to a college, but they did have the time to challenge us for playing a scrimmage game in another state – a game that was designed to expose a girl's softball talent so that she might be considered a candidate for a softball scholarship.

# COURT DATES BEGIN

In the next couple of days we made an appointment with an attorney who had some experience with civil rights violations. I explained that the game was in West Virginia and why we went there and played. The attorney secured the Michigan High School Athletic Association's by-laws and rulebook. The attorney did some extreme research on discrimination and due process. He informed us that they had no right to suspend her from the team without a hearing. This was a public school supported by tax money, and they had to abide by the due process laws.

We retained the lawyer. He went to circuit court and obtained a temporary restraining order, barring the coach and the high school from suspending the softball player. The hearing was scheduled for seven days later. The high school coach, the athletic director and the high school principal were all supposed to appear in court.

The judge had a copy of the high school association's manual of rules. He first swore in the high school coach. He asked the coach, "What do you determine is an organized game?" The coach answered, "As long as a score is kept on a game, this would be considered outside competition." The same question was put to the high school athletic director and the high school principal. All with the same answers – if a score is kept it is considered organized outside competition.

The judge then asked another question directed at the three high school officials: "If this girl's family had a family picnic and her father had his side of the family play his wife's side of the family in a softball game, and his daughter was to play three innings for each side of the family and a score was kept, would she be violating your school rules?" All three high school officials answered yes. The judge continued the restraining order and also ordered the high school officials to immediately restore the girl back to the team. "And she is to be playing as a regular first-stringer as she was before the suspension."

The few days following this court decision were filled with irrational anger from other high school coaches in the area. One of my players quit her high school team because of all the flack she was getting from the high school coach. Her high school coach had threatened to suspend her if she played or showed up for any of our practices. Two of my other players complained to me that they were being benched on their high school team, not allowed to play in the starting positions that they had played in before this court case. Another player complained that her high school coach repeatedly came into the shower area while the girls were showering after a game, in order to discuss their next practice. The player told me that her high school team thought she was gay, because she had a girl friend who was always hanging around her high school team, wherever they went. I thought to myself, "What is happening in this maze of problems? Are these high school coaches jealous or are they very possessive of their players, or is it me –

because I'm a guy coaching girls' softball? Why should these girls be exposed to this kind of complaining?"

Some of the players' parents and I had a meeting at the store. As we sat down at this meeting, we were looking for answers and direction. They asked me what I really thought about all of this – and did some of these girls really have a chance at a college softball scholarship? I told them that people were trying to derail us. We were just a local team ushering in a winning machine with superior talent, and our presence was well noted in the media. Apparently, this was not welcomed by some high school coaches and parents, mostly because their daughters were not part of this team, made up of a bunch of girls who displayed durability, a fierce competitiveness, consistency and spirit. I was pegged as a hard-ass perfectionist coach who assembled a demolition team from local mediocre softball talent.

I added, "As far as the players' college visions go, some have a good chance and some need more work. But most of all, they don't need silly jealousy and intimidation by stupid and discriminating rules from the Michigan High School Athletic Association, which states that boys playing high school baseball can play outside softball competitively, while the girls can't play in any outside softball competition." I told the parents that I would consult the lawyer again about the intimidation. Before the two-hour meeting ended, I asked the parents what they thought about our going to Federal Court to challenge these discriminatory rules. Their reply: "You're the coach."

Off I went to see the lawyer again. We talked and agreed that our players were being harassed. You didn't need glasses to see through the tactics some were using to derail us.

# ON TO FEDERAL COURT

The lawyer filed a restraining order in the Federal Court in Detroit. The order contained 22 pages of complaints and cases cited. We also used the testimony from the previous case in Circuit Court. The Federal judge agreed and ordered the Michigan High School Athletic Association and the four high schools involved to refrain from suspending any players on our team who were playing high school softball.

I went out to watch one of my players play in her next high school game following the court order. I noticed a vehicle with two men inside parked near the playing field. I was told they were Federal Marshals who were making sure that the judge's order was being enforced. Could this be happening? Apparently, some high school coaches and fans could not accept the fact that our team was no mediocre organization; we were a winning machine, a bunch of girls made up of fierce competitors, durability, consistency, and spirit. And I was pegged as a hard-ass perfectionist coach trying to dominate girls' softball. All this creative vocabulary would only give us a new appetite to improve.

In the next couple of weeks, the high school atmosphere settled down and our girls' team was 6-0 in one league and 5-0 in the other.

With the mounting attorney fees and store vendors' bills came mounting concerns of how to keep afloat. I had an idea, but it was an idea I wasn't too proud of carrying out.

# THE BIG MISTAKE

I started to falsify my financial statement in order to secure credit from vendors. I was falsifying my available cash and receivables to persuade vendors to ship merchandise to me on an open account. Merchandise started coming in every day – lots of it! It had been two more weeks now, and I was receiving so much merchandise that I needed a second building for storage, so I rented another small building to store all the sporting goods. Soon, I was selling merchandise to smaller sport shops, cheaper than they could buy it from their vendors, because I wasn't paying the bills for this merchandise. I was even taking merchandise across the border to Windsor, Ontario. Cash was plentiful now. I started to pay a little on the older bills and stalled off the newer vendors.

Our girls' team was winning – we weren't just winning, we were blowing teams away, 22-1, 20-3. We were undefeated in both leagues and racked up a 14-0 record in one league and were 18-0 in the other. And four of our best players were still in high school! All of this really worried me. As we continued to demolish local teams, fans and parents of these teams boycotted my store and continued to intimidate our team. However, a local sports writer wrote an article in the *Detroit News* saying, "If you have a young girl playing sports, take her to see the second-base person for All Sports." This helped us to erase the negative attitude toward our team. We were not going to lose focus on how we came together and advanced our skills to pursue our goals. We would not retreat from this.

Some parents and fans from the other teams were asking themselves, "How can this Sport Shop financially support all of this: team uniforms, legal fees, traveling to tournaments, and players visiting colleges?" They knew there wasn't that much business going through my store. Rumors became conclusions of an accurate assessment. Where was all this money coming from? I wrestled with this tirelessly; a demeanor of success was a false image I was displaying. The team didn't understand and I didn't explain. They didn't care – they just wanted to play softball. The girls paid no attention to the business rumors. Indisputably, I was their coach and together we had come a long way. If I could play a part in sending some of the girls to college by way of a softball scholarship, nothing else seemed to matter. Maybe this gave me the flexibility to survive the results.

The end of the school year was approaching, and more parents were showing up at my shop with teenage daughters hoping to satisfy their visions of playing softball while honing their skills to become tomorrow's college stars. However, the tranquility of the scene wasn't without cost.

It was mind-boggling – we now had 42 players in our organization with no defections. It was a strange twist for a bunch of girls who not so long ago had lacked the respect of those who watched them play. One more girl dropped out of her high school team to climb aboard the All Sports express.

I had to call a team meeting at the store to sort out all these players and how to fit them all into our two leagues. I told the team, "I will never cut you from the team. You, however, could ultimately cut yourself by not giving 100% to the team and your teammates." We now had a competitive balance to choose the best of both teams to compete for top tournament play. There was no mistaking – we had the ability to emerge from the pack, which initiated a dilemma – winning in a convincing fashion. Another few days went by. We were 29-1 in both leagues. We began to make our mark. We were really for real.

Time spent with my wife was little, and the softball team took over my life. I was receiving inquiries from college coaches. Many of those college coaches requested videos of my players. We were good, but I wouldn't let up. Practices were long and some criticism came from parents, but never from the players. Some of our opponents on the field were complaining that we were too professional. We now racked up 36 wins against just one loss. We gained some new fans and captured their hearts and respect. There was no one laughing at this team. The laughter that was once directed at these players became cheers that confirmed a loyal following.

School was out, and our high school players emerged as another spark in our accelerated season. We had to make plans for college visits, especially for the seniors who had just graduated and the juniors who would be seniors in the fall. These players were eligible to talk to college coaches.

# INDIANA TRIP

On the upcoming weekend, we were going to Southern Indiana University. I was taking five players to audition for the college coach. We left in the early evening on Friday and spent Friday night just outside of the campus of Southern Indiana. On Saturday, the girls went through their workouts for the coach. The coach was amazed at how these girls handled themselves on the ball field, She personally showed the players around the campus. After the campus tour, the coach and I talked. She informed me that she had some funds available and that she was very much interested. I told her I would discuss the visit with the players. We started back to Michigan on Saturday evening. While en route, we discussed the college. The girls said there wasn't too much of a campus – it was a small college. When we arrived back home, I asked the players to take the time to write a thank you note to the college coach. I was conditioning the girls to appreciate these college visits.

There was one thing that bothered me about these college coaches. Some of them would ask the players if they would walk on the team as a freshman, then the college could free up some scholarship money for the next year. Well, if a player was on the team as a sophomore and the college still couldn't offer them scholarship money, the players would be put in a bind. If a player chose to leave the college because no funds were available, she would be ineligible to play as a junior in a new school. As a result, the player would wind up coming onto the college team as a senior. Not too many coaches would want to invest scholarship money on a one-year player. Some colleges have political maneuvers that can confuse the players in the process.

The next morning just before I opened the sport shop, I was approached by a man who identified himself as a reporter for a local newspaper. He asked me, "Is there a story here?" I looked up, "What do you mean?" He answered, "Well, here we have a highly visible girls' softball team supported by your sport shop in games, tournaments, college visits and court cases - a sport shop that is financially fumbling." I replied, "You seem to know a lot about my business and my team." He answered, "I know enough to notice UPS delivering an overwhelming amount of merchandise that doesn't all seem to stay in your store. Do you want to talk about this?" I just looked at him and replied, "Do you have a daughter who wishes she could play on this team or do you have a personal version you're chasing?" I wished him a good day and went about my business in the store.

# LIMPE THE CAT

That evening as I was taking some empty boxes out the back door to the dumpster, I noticed a calico cat lying on the grass. She was in pain. I thought a car had hit her. I picked her up and drove to the nearest veterinary clinic that I could find open. I took the cat in to the vet. He told me her pelvis was injured and I asked him to fix her. He wanted a deposit, because people would leave pets that were injured or sick and never come back for them. I left $200 with the vet and told him to call me when she was ready. The next afternoon they called. She had had surgery on her pelvis and they told me that she could never have kittens. I agreed to pick her up the next day. I guessed having a cat in the store wouldn't be too bad.

So I was off to the pet store for a litter box, food and water bowls, cat food and a soft basket to sleep in. The first couple of days in the store, the cat was always hiding. She got used to the store and my team loved having the cat to play with. But she did have a habit of hiding behind the coat racks and when someone came into the store, she would jump out and scare them. She was funny and fun. The cat was an outlet for me at times; she made me laugh and smile.

We were practicing and winning games, gaining new fans and followers. There was still the parade of resentment from other teams and their fans, but still fans applauded our ability to win. We were starting to silence some of the verbal and jealous abuse of some players and fans.

We entered our team in a couple of softball tournaments in other cities in Michigan. Both tournaments were satisfying. We lost one game and won a total of nine games in the two tournaments and took home both first place trophies. With league and tournament play we were 58-3. Not bad for a team of unknown nobodies assembled a year ago. The trophies began to take their place in the store.

Three of the senior girls on the team were contacted by college coaches. The end result was that three of our players were going to attend a Division I college on a full ride scholarship. The team was pumped up and I was so proud of them. We were now poised for the National Championship. It was only 11 weeks to Nationals. We had our credentials as the team to watch. We had our sights on Tullahoma, Tennessee, the site of the Girls' National Tournament.

# THE PHONE CALL

It was a warm Monday morning when I opened the store for business. I always fed the cat first and dealt with the litter box. The phone was ringing while I was taking the cat litter out the back door. Then it stopped. About ten minutes later it rang again. I answered; it was my attorney. He said that he had received a courtesy call from a U.S. Attorney informing him that I was the target of an investigation dealing with mail fraud. My heart started racing. I started to feel fear, then pain. My attorney said, "There's nothing anyone can do. Just go about your business and life, but do not order any new merchandise." He said that he would monitor their investigation and keep me informed. I just sat down at my desk. My mind overtook my body. You can't disarm the truth. The wheels of justice were starting to determine my fate. I now had to get in touch with the truth of my feelings. What did I expect? I had made some bad choices. There is no pouting in the corner – you work through all of it and prepare for the worst. I got through the day; there were no softball games or practices. Good! I wanted to be alone. That night I stayed late at the store, canceling some pending orders for merchandise.

The next day after closing the store, I left early to prepare for our softball game that night. The team sensed something was wrong. There was no "rah-rah – let's win!" and all the spirited talk that coaches usually show. The team never asked about anything and I didn't volunteer anything. We won the game. Two more players told me that colleges had contacted them. I really was happy for them and told the players that if they wanted to discuss these colleges, they could stop by the store. Tears were welling up in my eyes and I wouldn't release them. The players and I agreed to meet the next night at the store.

When I opened up the store the next morning, something wasn't right. I couldn't find "Limpe" the cat. I had named her Limpe because after her surgery she walked with a limp. I looked all over inside the store and went out the back door calling for her – no Limpe. I remembered that the day before when I was taking the cat litter out and the phone rang, I may have forgotten to shut the door completely. My anger was shielding my fear. She was gone. It had been a bad two days. I kept looking out the window for Limpe, and I left the back door open during the day in case she would return. As it turns out I never saw Limpe the cat again, but I had comfort in knowing that she was now in good health.

I started going through my mail – bills, bills, and more bills. Except for one letter from the U.S. Postal Inspector's Office. It was a subpoena to show up at the Post Office in Detroit to give handwriting samples. I called my attorney. He told me that I had to obey the subpoena. They wanted me to write things for them to compare with some purchase orders they had. I had six days to comply. I also received calls from two other stores that I had sold some merchandise to. The storeowners told me that two FBI agents were asking questions about some of their floor merchandise – questions such as, "Where did you buy some of this merchandise and would you provide the bills showing that you purchased these items and when?" These storeowners had also been subpoenaed to appear, to answer questions pertaining to their involvement with and relationship to me. The next few days I started to prepare myself for my appointment to give handwriting samples. Calculating my options regarding the softball team, the colleges, and the U.S. Justice Department, I came up with NONE.

The day came for me to produce myself to the postal authorities. For two hours I was writing sentences about ordering merchandise. I was reproducing my purchase orders for merchandise that I purchased with a blown up credit statement. They wanted to make sure that I was the one placing these orders. When I was finished, they politely thanked me, and I left to go back to the store.

Everyone grows up knowing about Santa Claus and Superman. We all at one time or another want to believe in these myths. We just need something to hang onto and I was hoping that this was going to work out some how and I would be alright.

"Tonight we have a softball game. And tonight I'm not going to be any different." The team knew I was back mentally. I was yelling at them for their little miscues on the field.

Sometimes fear creates energy. The laughter and tears we shared while assembling this team was giving me strength to move forward. I had players being embraced by college coaches. And I had players who were going to have the chance to further their education by playing softball and not waltzing into college on their parents' bankroll. I had players who were underdogs and outsiders in a wealthy society. We had girls who had become ladies for life's challenges. We were not just a softball team winning games. We were heroes to each other. This team would go on and we would go to Nationals. The sport shop was only a physical building that mirrored my mistakes – mistakes and blunders that would change my life forever. But other people's lives would be changed too. There would be stories to be told. The days ahead would convince me that the wrongdoing I had committed could not be covered up. But was I trying to make an excuse for failing the only real asset I had – myself? I made up my mind, "We will move forward together as a team, and on the way if a few girls emerge as college candidates for softball scholarships, this will help me to survive the storm ahead."

I also believed that since the State of Michigan had never produced a Girls' National Softball Championship, more people should take an active role in supporting an alliance with us to deliver this goal. Our softball practices became more intense and longer. There was no letting up. I tried to operate the sport shop as usual, but I must concede the fact that it was doomed to fail. I failed it. When I was in the store, I felt I was in lonely isolation, preparing myself for the response of the Department of Justice for my actions.

That night when I arrived home, there was a message to call my attorney. It was out of context for my attorney to call me at home, asking me to return his call that night. I slowly picked up the phone and dialed his home number. He answered. "They indicted you today on 17 counts of mail fraud." I had two days to turn myself in to the U.S. Marshal's office in Detroit, where I would be processed and taken before a Federal judge for arraignment. My stomach tightened, but I had known it would come to this. My lawyer advised me to ask for a court-appointed attorney, and plead mute at the arraignment. I needed a criminal attorney who worked the Federal courts, in my situation. I called my kids and went to each of their homes to explain what was happening and why. I then called my coach and asked him to assemble the team early the next morning. It was late Saturday night. I went back to the store and called my brothers to alert them to the agenda at hand. I then called my wife at work – she was on the afternoon shift. She was disappointed and I apologized for any embarrassment, now and in the future. I stayed at the store until the early morning hours, pondering what I was going to tell the team and my coach, who had been so dedicated to me. Finally, I went home to sleep for a couple of hours, and tried to freshen up for our 10:00 a.m. team meeting at the store.

Sometimes there are painful realities associated with success. Early Sunday morning, I stopped for coffee at the newspaper stand, thinking about what to say at this meeting with my players. As I flipped through the pages of the newspaper, there it was on page 3 – all about me: Local Coach Being Indicted For Mail Fraud. I only read the article once. That was enough. I opened the store, and shortly after, the players started showing up. My coach came in and walked up to me. "Did you see the newspaper?" I just nodded my head yes. The silence in the store created a small anxiety. When you were a child you sometimes pretended you were an adult. Now that you are an adult, this is one of those times you pretend you're a child. To be a child even takes courage. I said to myself, "Enough of this foolishness." I told my team, "Relax and be comfortable. I have something important to explain to you. Not too long ago, I made some bad business decisions relating to the sport shop. For this, I'm being charged with a crime. I will not deny these charges. There's going to be newspaper articles and people describing me as a criminal, and probably not fit to be your coach. Some people will judge me by my image of breaking the law. Some people will still judge me by substance. But what will always be important to me is that you remember the ultimate courage we shared together in the courts and on the playing field to emerge as the team you are today. We fought the platoons of the non-believers together. Through the courts we leveled the playing field so other girls can follow your road map. Now, through these same courts, I must take this journey. I will resolve this quickly. There will be no trial. You are the first to know that I will plead guilty. You will stay focused on playing softball and your grades in school. Tomorrow, we will practice as usual, only more intense, no letting up. This is no time for mutiny."

I spent the rest of the day pretending it was business as usual, but I was scared as I prepared myself for the verbal attack describing me in the days ahead. I planned on going to the Federal Building the next day to surrender and be processed for court.

The next morning I woke up early to prepare for my surrender to court. As I went out the door, there was no car. My car was gone – my wife's car was there, but not mine. I called the local police. They informed me that the car was repossessed by the bank. Why? I was current on my payments. I called the bank. Their answer to me was that they felt the account was in jeopardy because I was facing prison. So much for P.R. from one of the "Big Three." I borrowed my wife's car.

# VISIT TO THE FEDERAL BUILDING

I arrived at the Federal Building and reported to the U.S. Marshal's office. I was fingerprinted, mug shots were taken, and I was escorted upstairs to Federal court. The judge asked me if I understood the charges against me. I answered "Yes." I stood mute of the charges and asked the judge to appoint an attorney for me. I requested a personal bond, and the judge granted it to me. I then was escorted to the stairs to Pre-Trial Services. This department was helpful in explaining what was expected of me. No traveling outside of Michigan without their permission and no traveling to Canada. They informed me that a court-appointed attorney would be contacting me. Before returning home with the car, I made a stop at the sport shop. Surprise number two for the day: my store was padlocked with a notice slapped on the door. The court placed a lien on my store and its contents. I then drove to the warehouse that I used to store merchandise. Surprise number three: padlocked, same notice.

I drove home. I relived my morning with my wife. She felt bad, but we both knew that it was all on my shoulders, a sobering reminder of what loneliness is. Again, I was looking for my fear to give me energy.

I needed transportation, so I went to my bank with the little money I had in the checking account. Perhaps a cheap used car was the answer. Surprise number four: my account was frozen pending a garnishment hearing. One of my vendors executed their judgment. Once again, I returned home. This time the tears that were sometimes in my eyes came out. I thought to myself "All this timing of freezing me in my tracks. This took some planning. Was I this important?" I remembered reading about the arrest of some drug dealers who weren't rendered this type of pre-verdict. Somebody assembled quite a cast of characters for my derailment. I called my coach and he gave me a ride to our practice that evening.

When we arrived at the field for practice, the girls were all done with their stretch exercises and eager to practice. They knew what I was feeling. No one said anything about anything except our regular softball practice talk. There was a full contingent of players and more parents than usual. Knowing that there was a good possibility that I wouldn't be their coach too long from now, I hurried through more fundamentals and crammed in extra batting practices. I was also more verbal, more deliberate, and more intense. If I was going down, I wanted this team running on high octane and thinking of winning that national championship. A national championship would mean so much on a softball player's resume for a college scholarship. I pushed and I pushed hard at practice. After practice, we had our usual team meeting. This time I invited the parents that had shown up for practice to join our team meeting. This was a first for me – I always conducted the team meetings with only players and coaches. Everyone was silent. I looked at everyone and said, "I will answer any questions from anyone here about softball and where this team is going, and of course about my situation with my Federal indictment." One parent said, "The girls have worked so hard and have come so far; we want to help. What can we do?" I answered in a very high-spirited voice, "Stand by these girls. Keep supporting their goals. They're good kids and they not only have defeated opponents on the playing field, they defeated the disadvantages of poverty and discrimination. They are young girls playing a game a softball and winning like ladies." Another parent asked, "Do you think you will have to go away?" I answered, "That's a good possibility." Some of the players took a few steps back and turned around. There were tears. I motioned for the parents to go to their side and turn them back to face this meeting. I looked at my team and said," A while back you guys walked into my shop and asked me to coach you, to help you learn the game of softball. People were laughing at your playing ability. I agreed, and here we are, poised for a National Championship and no one's laughing anymore at you. Now, I want to walk into your hearts and minds and I want you to promise me you will continue to stay focused on your school responsibilities and your softball goals. This will be my beacon for what's ahead for me. Tomorrow we have a game to play, and next week two of you guys are expected at a college campus. And I don't want you guys to say 'we will try.' Trying is for losers. Trying implies the possibility of losing. Losers only try. Winners never try. Winners only win. And you are winners. See you at the game tomorrow."

My coach gave me a ride home, and I told him that he would need help. We talked about asking one of the parents to help coach. We wanted to prepare for whatever we had to deal with.

That night I called my oldest daughter. I knew she had an older second car. I needed transportation. She agreed. Now I had some transportation.

I tried to watch a little TV, but there was a fog in my brain and I couldn't connect my thoughts. There was no sport shop to go to. My car was gone as well as my bank account. I had very little cash. Fate has a way of slamming you down, just when you think you're getting ahead. I guess twists of fate make you mistrust your instincts. I was trying to be truthful with myself but it's a slippery thing. It got me thinking again, truth isn't necessarily what you see, but how you see it. I was wrong and it was time to ante up and get all of this over with. The doorbell rang. It's 10:00 p.m. – okay – I answered it. A man politely asks, "Are you Mr. ___?"

"Yes, I am."

"This is for you."

I looked. My wife was divorcing me. When it rains, it pours. What next? I read the divorce suit. The web of disappointments was spinning larger. I guess I expected it. My wife shouldn't have to go through all this. I waited for her to come home from her afternoon shift. When she arrived, I had a false smile to greet her. She knew I had received the papers. Another court to attend to. We sat down and talked. I acknowledged my shortcomings and my failure of being a good husband the past two years. The sport shop and the softball team did her in. Make no mistake; I failed her. We discussed what would be fair. I told her there would be no objections from me. She paid all the bills and house payments most of the last three years. She knew I had no funds. I agreed to forfeit any rights to the house, cars, and household items. I just wanted a bed, a couple of pieces of furniture and a little cash to get me through wherever I was going. This was a smooth arrangement with no objections. We both shed some tears while hugging each other. For a while my fear of everything that was going on began to subside.

Morning came. I needed to look for a small apartment. The phone rang. My court-appointed attorney summoned me to her office. I arrived at her office and was greeted by a young girl – a girl that I could easily describe as a young softball player on my team. But this was my court-appointed attorney. We sat down. She walked me through the 21-page indictment. They even had an FBI agent listed as a customer who made a purchase at my shop and paid by check. I guess that produced the answer to where I banked. She asked me if I had any questions. I said no. She said, "Did you do all this?" I answered "Yes." She showed me handwriting samples that I had given at the Postal Inspector's office; they matched signatures on credit applications and financial statements. My attorney asked me what I wanted to do. I said, "Let's plead guilty and ask for a lesser sentence." She said she would talk to the U.S. Attorney assigned to the case. She also recommended that I get my personal affairs in order and prepare for the worst. She also advised me to seek letters from my associates attesting to my character. A judge reads all letters on behalf of a defendant. I went home and called my coach and briefed him on what had taken place at my attorney's office. He said that he would pursue and devote the necessary time to acquiring letters of character on my behalf. I thanked him, but reminded him that I was not to be the obvious subject of focus here. The players and the National Tournament must not be neglected.

When I arrived at the ball field for our game, I noticed a few more spectators than usual. There also was heckling from a few fans voicing their opinions of my indictment. We won the game, but the players weren't that hungry for the win. It was like they were going through the motions of winning the game, and miscues were made. We had our team meeting after the game. I informed the team that we would be practicing three days that week at a different playing site. There was too much distraction from fans and there was too much work to be done – we were looking a little sloppy. We'd all been through a lot this season. There seemed to be a lot of dead tongues. We were much better than this.

The next day I found a small, inexpensive apartment not far from everything. This was good enough for me. I ordered a phone and had the utilities turned on. I notified the court of my new address and phone number. I now had time on my hands to crank up the softball team and escort a couple more players to college auditions. I wanted to stay busy and keep my mind off the courts.

At the next practice, I told the team that our base sliding was lazy, as well as our hustle. Our spirited instinct was lacking. I told them I would not accept this sudden laid-back attitude. I lined the players up on the base line and held a baseball bat five feet from the base, waist-high. One by one, I shouted, "Run as fast as you can and slide under the bat to the base." No one hit the bat. Suddenly their sliding improved. I wanted the players to get mad at me. I didn't want sympathy. I yelled at them, "All of a sudden we have cement feet running the bases. So let's start running the outfield three times around and hustle back here." We took batting practice and worked on defensive situations. At our team meeting after practice, I explained to my players that, "when you take the field in the Nationals, you're going to be playing against the best each state has sent to the tournament. You will have to be mentally prepared and physically ready. Tomorrow we will practice again. I want you to show up motivated to practice hard. Don't pretend this is practice as usual. The Nationals are approaching. You must take care of business on the field and I'll take care of my off-the-field business. You don't have to drive a nice car and have a credit card in your purse to be somebody. You players have proven this. You are a class act fueled by energy and spirit. You're a rare accomplishment in our society. Believe in each other. Sometimes definition is better than greatness. Sometimes having both will expand your opportunities. I believe this is you. See you tomorrow at practice."

The next morning my attorney called to inform me that the U.S. Attorney would accept a plea of guilty to two counts of mail fraud with a maximum sentence of 18 months. I told her, "Let's get it over with." She said that I would have to appear before a Federal judge and enter my plea for the record. I agreed.

I was trying to feel comfortable in my small apartment, but I couldn't identify myself with anything. All the pictures and furniture of my old home were missing.

The next day at practice I didn't exhibit any let-up. I pushed the girls at practice and drilled them on the fundamentals. More games are lost by simple mistakes on the field than by the big "one plays" that people remember. I kept driving into their minds: "Winners never try. Losers try. Winners win."

The usual hecklers didn't show up at our practice that day. There were very little distractions. This was a very good practice. I informed the team that we were adding another coach to our staff – it was one of the parents. He was very much interested in the team and was a loyal fan. He was a welcomed addition to our team. I told the team that we would not play in the State Tournament. We already qualified for Nationals, "so let's not play spoilers or maybe beat a team that might have a chance to qualify for Nationals by winning the tournament."

# TRIP TO IOWA

That weekend we were taking two players to Iowa. This time, my finances weren't available for the trip. The rest of the team would be practicing and my two coaches would continue working on their rough edges. The Friday before leaving for Iowa, the father of one of the players making the trip to Iowa asked to meet with me for breakfast. While we were discussing the college visit to Iowa, he handed me an envelope with money in it. The father was aware of my financial situation. He wanted to help. He told me to "show them a nice time" and thanked me for all my past efforts toward the team.

That afternoon, the two players and I made the 11-hour journey to Ames and Iowa City. The 2:00 p.m. Saturday workout came. The players went through their usual practice for the coaches. Both players showed good energy and did a lot of the right things on the softball field. The coaches at both colleges were extremely pleasant and showed the girls a well-remembered afternoon. The coaches complimented me on their ability, and they showed a much-advanced interest in the two girls. The coaches asked me several questions, especially about the girls being away from home. This was important, because if they were on scholarship and felt homesick and left the program, their scholarship would be lost to the college. I sensed that these coaches really wanted the players, and by talking to some of the people in the area, I learned that people didn't even lock their doors at night. The girls liked the coaches at both colleges, as well as the campuses.

We started back to Michigan on Sunday morning, with a stop at the college bookstore. The girls wanted t-shirts. I bought the shirts with the money given to me earlier by the father of one of the girls. On the way home, we talked about our team, the college coaches and the coming National Softball Tournament. Then the conversation turned to me. The team never talked with me about my indictment and court date. But this time, one of the players asked if I was worried. I answered that I was, but not scared. This talk was very unusual for me, because I always had felt the softball team was a temporary sanctuary from all of my court mess. The two players said that the whole team was very concerned, but everyone was afraid to discuss it or ask me anything about it. However, I did tell them that I was ashamed and concerned about the unknown outcome to follow. One of the players said to me, "Just the other night you told us that you don't have to drive a nice car and have a credit card in your purse in order to be somebody. Well, *you* don't have to drive a nice car and have a credit card in your wallet to be a somebody." I smiled. "Let's talk softball."

A coach is supposed to keep a certain distance of one's feelings for a team, but this team and I had bonded. We had bonded with respect and loyalty. The wins and losses were just the physical results of this bond. The real results were that we all shared a common sense of mystery of what goes on in a person's heart, of why people do what they do. It was a bond about little people making a connection against the hazards of life.

Tomorrow would be another day, another practice and another game. With each practice and game, I knew the time was approaching when there would be no more practices or games for me.

# BACK TO REALITY

That night when I arrived home at my apartment, there was a phone message from my young attorney. The court date to enter my guilty plea before the judge was in four days. She informed me that there were several letters on my behalf that she had sent over to the judge's clerk. She told me that the judge reads all letters sent on behalf of a defendant. She also inquired about how the team was doing. I invited her to join in one of our practices. I told her that she could fit in with these young girls. They were a team of phenomenal softball ability, but not short on feminine attraction. My lawyer declined the invitation, but acknowledged the compliment. There was so much to do and my time was getting short. My lawyer and I knew that there wasn't a good chance of my receiving probation. She told me that judges were coming down hard on paper crimes – "be prepared."

There were no practices or games for the next two days. I took a drive by the sport shop. It was silent. The windows were dirty and the padlock was still on the door. Everything inside was intact. Limpe the cat was still no where to be seen. The parking lot was empty. I went a few doors down to the coffee shop, read the paper and talked to a couple of the regulars. No one asked about the court situation. They all knew and allowed me that respect. The owners of the coffee shop owed me a small amount of money for some lettered t-shirts. They didn't know whom to pay. I just told them that if they ever saw a limping cat walking around, feed her and find her a home. I marked his bill PAID IN FULL. Coming back to this scenery wasn't helping. As I left, he marked my bill PAID.

That afternoon, I called my kids and invited them out to eat. We drove a distance for dinner. I just wanted to be someplace away and new to me. It was a nice dinner. I told my kids that I was sorry for not always being around the last few years to do things together. I made no excuses and they weren't looking for any. We talked and shared the past and looked to better days ahead. I told them that if I had to go away for a while, not to come and visit me. Let this part of my life be mine alone to deal with.

The next day was game day. I spent the early part of the day visiting my coach at work. He took his lunch break and we talked about the team doing something away from softball. It had been a tense season so far, and we both knew the worst was yet to come. We talked about taking the team to Cedar Point in Ohio. I was confident that I could receive permission to travel to Ohio. So we agreed to talk to the team after that night's game.

We won the game 10-2 and there were more than the usual hecklers directing their remarks about me: "Criminals don't belong coaching young girls." After the game, we walked to the deep outfield to have our team meeting. I let my coach do the talking about the game and the Cedar Point trip. The players were excited. We made plans to leave for Cedar Point Saturday morning. It was nice to see the team happy and talkative.

The next morning I prepared myself for court. I arrived at the Federal Court in Detroit about 1:00 p.m. for my 1:30 p.m. plea. My attorney arrived 15 minutes later. We discussed my guilty plea and how I would answer the judge. My stomach started to tighten up. We walked into the courtroom, sat down and waited for our case to be called. Shortly, the Federal judge called our case number. We both came forward and stood in front of the judge. The U.S. Attorney read the charges. The judge asked if we had worked out a plea bargain. My attorney answered yes. The judge looked at me and asked if I understood this plea bargain, with the potential of 18 months incarceration and five years of probation. I answered, "Yes." He asked if anyone promised me anything for pleading guilty. I answered "No." The judge responded, "Very well, I will accept your guilty plea and schedule sentencing for 18 days from now. I also am ordering a pre-sentence report from the Probation Department." The judge extended my bail. We left the courtroom. My attorney advised me to organize my personal affairs. Then I went upstairs to the Probation Department. They asked me a lot of questions about my past life and education, and told me a probation officer would be visiting me shortly at my apartment. There was a little relief in my tightened stomach. This was finally coming to an end, and I would prepare myself for the next court date – sentencing.

That night I called my players and cancelled Friday's practice and told them to be ready for a 6 a.m. departure for the three-hour ride to Cedar Point, Ohio. I also called my coach and the two new coaches we had chosen to help out with the team, asking them to meet at my apartment the next night. The next day I did a little shopping – some pop, beer and munchies for our coaches' meeting. I also called the U.S. Probation

Department for permission to travel to the Cleveland, Ohio area for our Cedar Point outing.

That night at the meeting, I expressed my wishes that the team have a really good time at Cedar Point. I gave the coaches some money to purchase tickets for Cedar Point and for refreshments. I also passed out funds for gasoline expenses. We were taking four cars; the three coaches and I would oversee the trip from start to the return trip home. I told the coaches to let the girls have fun, and if they were noisy and loud at the park, so be it. "Don't be parents; stay back and just keep them in the boundaries of good wholesome fun."

Saturday morning came. We stocked up on coffee, donuts, and soda pop for the ride. It was a beautiful May day, and everyone enjoyed the trip and the amusement park. We only had to shy away about 16 young boys from pursuing the girls' phone numbers, which wasn't a surprise. I tried to blend in with the team, the laughter and excitement. Their smiles were different from the smiles of a winning softball team.

Sunday was another day off for the team. I wanted to see some friends and make contact with some of my nieces and nephews. This took most of the day, and that Sunday evening I visited my three brothers. Everyone knew the turmoil I was in. No one preached at me. They were concerned about tomorrow and getting all this behind us.

Monday came. We had a game to play that night. We were playing a team that was nested in $2^{nd}$ place behind us. They had only two losses. Both teams were up for the challenge. There was no score until the $3^{rd}$ inning. We were up to bat and had a runner on first with no outs. Our batter hit a hard grounder to $3^{rd}$ base. The $3^{rd}$ base girl had to back up a couple of steps to handle that hard-hit ball and she threw the ball to the $2^{nd}$ base girl who was standing on the base waiting for the ball.

Our base runner slid into the base and knocked the 2$^{nd}$ base girl over, and she dropped the ball. Everyone was safe. The other team's fans' temperature and mood started to react. The heckling was strong and very verbal. That inning we scored four runs. When the inning ended, their 2$^{nd}$ base girl walked toward our 2$^{nd}$ base girl as we were taking the field to play defense. She bumped into our player and they exchanged words mouth to mouth. Their fans got into the yelling. My coach yelled out to their fans, "If your 2$^{nd}$ base girl knew how to cover the base correctly, she probably wouldn't have dropped the ball!"

This only added fuel to the fire. Their fans were yelling, "At least our manager isn't going to prison!" All of our players gathered around the pitcher's mound and yelled, "Look at the score: 4-0!" I instructed our team to sit on the bench "Our team is not taking the field with this undesirable behavior from that team's fans." The umpire replied, "There's nothing I can do about the heckling by the team's fans." I asked, "What about their 2$^{nd}$ base girl bumping into our player? You as an umpire should remove a player who physically exhibits poor sportsmanlike conduct. You also have the authority to clear the fans from the stands and into the parking lot." He answered, "Let's play ball!" I suggested to him that he give the other team a warning, because "I will not subject these girls to any more abusive behavior in this league." He said, "Are you going to take the field and play ball?" I answered, "Are you going to give a warning to that team and their fans?" He answered, "No!" I responded, "If you can't stop the hostile atmosphere that's being displayed toward my team, then my team will not take the field." The umpire forfeited the game to the other team and gave us a loss. We walked off the field to our bench. The other team and their fans were displaying their happiness and yelling "We're Number One!" They were still one game behind us in the standings. The last time we played them we had beaten them, 11-2.

We had our team meeting after the fans left. I told my team, "That team did not beat you. They suffered a bigger loss than they could imagine. The real story is that you know where the finish line is, and how to get there. Forget this game and that team and all the other fans who are blind with jealousy. They know we're the goods. What they don't know is that emotion can be more fuel for strength. When you guys stand out as an impressive team, you become targets for petty jealousy and bad behavior. You have won many admirers, both younger and older than you. Don't lose focus and the tempo of your journey. Go home happy and proud!"

The next day I spent a good part of the morning with the league director. I told him, "I don't care about the forfeit loss. However, I am very concerned about the attitude of some players and fans toward our team." The league director agreed and promised to call a league meeting. I called my two coaches that night and we set up a meeting of our own the next night. We met at the usual coffee shop. We talked about future practices and games. I told my coaches to brace for some dicey days ahead. "Our team is being stressed in many ways. That line between past and present is getting very real. We are too good for the competition around us and I am saddled with some heavy baggage. We all are targets of the hecklers. The dilemma probably won't change and neither will we. You coaches must carry on. The team's tempo must remain strong with consistency and spirit. Their playing ability and sportsmanship will silence all the hostility. The girls have demonstrated that they're a product of courage. They have come a long way this past year, and they know where they are going. So you coaches fuel up and hop on for the ride!"

The next day I was informed by the league director of a league meeting in two days. The league director and I agreed that our coaches would not attend this meeting. The day of the league meeting, we conducted our usual long practice. We pushed the players to their limits of batting and fielding, running bases and working on game situations. We practiced until dark. No one complained. This team liked the hard work. They knew that they were admired by the same fans who used to laugh at their playing a year ago.

The next night we played a league game. We won 7-0; no heckling and no unsportsmanlike conduct. We could have won 20-0, but we wanted to start playing everyone on the team. We had to prepare the whole team, not just 10 or 11 key players. When you're in a national tournament and lose a game, sometimes you play 6 games in one day. The National Tournament was a double elimination tournament. I instructed my coaches: "We're not interested in humiliating teams and running up a high score of runs. Let's keep winning, but play everyone. Let's travel to the Nationals 20 players strong."

The next two days were off days; no practice and no games. On the second day off I received a call from my attorney. My throat got heavy and my tight stomach told me compliance was at hand. I didn't know if I would be taken away at sentencing or be given a time to report to prison. This was going to be a long and busy week. My ex-wife had called and told me that a probation officer was at her house asking her about me and our years of marriage. The officer asked her if I had ever hit her or had a drinking problem. Of course my ex-wife and I knew those answers. I never smoked or ever experienced being drunk in my life. I also have never hit a woman. The most I ever yelled was at my softball team. I still had that intimidating feeling about all this. My marriage had failed and I was facing a Federal judge for sentencing. It was ante-up time.

I had a week to repair any burned bridges. How do you save face in the process, or do you just surrender to guilt and try to move on? Move on to where? My attorney advised me to prepare a statement before the judge. She also informed me that the U.S. Attorney would issue a statement at my sentencing. The fear that seemed to disable me was getting to be my frequent companion, yet it challenged me. I also had 23 young softball players poised for a national softball tournament. I had learned more from these young girls playing softball than those who claim to know life's secrets and are eager to share their knowledge for a price.

We had 2 games that week and 2 practices. The other coaches and I knew what had to be done. We would not let up the pace and be distracted. We had to come from a 3-run deficit in the first game to win it, 8-4. We also won the second game, 7-1. Everyone was getting playing time, our tempo of winning was in high confidence and we were capturing more adult support. We also noticed that we were starting to garner more support from a lot of young girls. The hecklers were silent and we even had requests for autographs from little girls and boys. Our girls seemed embarrassed to be signing autographs for little girls. The local newspapers were inking us with some good articles. Maybe the meeting between the league director and teams had something to do with this. I also think our cast of characters was winning the hearts of the younger girls, who were just starting to learn the game of softball.

We were all starting to share a common sense of what was happening. No one had waved a magic wand to assemble a girls' softball team with so much phenomenal success. There were no pictures of these girls on bubble gum cards, but there were and always would be pictures in everyone's memory of how these girls emerged from a nobodies list and from adversity to make this leap to supremacy in girls' softball. Since the past fall we had won 68 games while losing only 8 games. Not bad for a team that consisted of mostly girls who emerged from poverty and discrimination. We were ready for wherever the teams came from to the National Tournament, and for whatever their story was.

I had three days until my sentencing in Federal Court. I gave the team a day off and we held practice the day before my court date. That night after practice the coaches and I held a meeting at the usual coffee shop. I told the coaches that I didn't know what to expect at my sentencing – that my lawyer had told me that when you receive prison time, the judge usually gives you a few days to report. I had a little money left; I gave some of it to the coaches for the motel bills during the National Tournament and to provide some of the girls with better shoes and new softball mitts. My first coach, who had traveled this journey of softball with me for most of the time, offered to appear in court with me at my sentencing. I told him I needed to do this alone. The judge had all those letters on my behalf from friends, players and parents. By now, I thought, the judge had made up his mind.

Nighttime came at my apartment. I was alone, trying not to think about the next day's court date. My stomach was too tight. I couldn't sleep. I lay awake, inventing thoughts about tomorrow. After about five hours of sleep, I woke up, showered and tried to eat something. With no appetite and a nervous stomach, I started out for downtown Detroit. Parking near the Federal Building was $6. I just wanted to get this over with. I went through security and up to the third floor. I slowly entered the courtroom and sat down. I looked for my attorney, but she hadn't arrived yet. There were other offenses being sentenced before mine. Finally my attorney arrived. She sat next to me and asked what I was going to say before the judge. I told her that I wanted to make it simple and direct. About fifteen minutes later our case was called. The judge asked if all parties were ready for sentencing. The Assistant U.S. Attorney replied, "Yes," and my attorney responded, "We're ready, your honor." The judge acknowledged the many letters on my behalf. The judge said, "I want to ask you - what happened to all the money that didn't find its way to your creditors?" My attorney replied to the judge, "Your honor, most of his funds went to support a girls' softball program and he also used poor judgment. He admits this and he's sorry." The judge then said, "According to the probation report he has no car, no home, no bank accounts. The Probation Department made a thorough investigation of his finances. I can't even fine this defendant for his actions." The judge then asked me what I wanted to say before he passed sentence. I answered, "I want to thank the court for providing me with an attorney. I also admit that I made some bad choices that I can't undo. I'm sorry and I should have known better." I paused. The U.S. Attorney then said, "A lot of vendors didn't get paid because of his mistakes." The judge paused. "I hereby remand you to the U.S. Department of Corrections where you will serve a year and a day. Upon your release, you will serve five years of probation. You will be notified when to report in a few days by the Department of Corrections."

My attorney and I walked out into the court hall. She knew I was holding back a big tear, slowly giving way down the side of my nose. My attorney said that she thought the judge was fair and that she would stay in touch with me while I was in prison. She also said, "Now is the time to think about yourself and prepare for your notice of surrender." I thanked her and told her I would miss my kids and the team. I also said, "I'm prepared to pay my debt to society." I then took the slow ride home. My stomach felt a little better, so I stopped at the coffee shop for lunch. I informed some of my friends at the coffee shop of the results of my sentence. A couple of the guys offered some funds to be deposited in my commissary account at the prison. I wasn't too talkative, but I thanked them for the gesture, and said I would be fine. I just felt like seeing a movie by myself. Sometimes I can relax at the movies. I found myself watching a sad movie and left before it ended. I went home, called my caching staff and gave them the news. We talked and I asked them for a meeting the next night after practice.

# GETTING READY

The next morning I spent looking over personal bills and obligations. Later, I made myself go to the field for softball practice. Before we started practice, I called a meeting with the team and the coaching staff. I told them, "We need to prepare for the National Tournament. This includes playing all the players more often. We're going to focus on getting everyone ready, even if it means losing some games. Forget about winning or losing now; it's more important that everyone is sharp and fit. The Nationals can be a real test of durability. You may play 8-12 games in three days. I want everyone to support each other's role in this game plan. We need to prepare a total team, not just 10 players."

No one, as usual, said a word. I know they were waiting for me to say something about the previous day's court sentencing; they wanted to hear it from me. I informed them that shortly I would not be with them physically for the remainder of the season. I also said, "I will always remain with you in many other ways. Let's get down to practice now." We broke from the meeting into some extreme batting practice followed by hard base-running and infield and outfield drills. We played two games that week, and split with a 6-4 win and a 5-3 loss. The enthusiasm was good, but it was empty. It was like going through the motions without that intimidating spirit.

We scheduled a Sunday practice. I really pushed the players at practice. I told them that I sensed a let-up on their deliberate spirit of winning. I said, "Don't compromise all we have been through because of my situation. It will be a lot easier for me to face the next year ahead if you guys keep the spirit and continue to support each other. I can do my thing knowing that you will carry on what we worked for together. You guys are too important to each other, and to me, to let my mistakes change our course. Have faith in your coaches; I will start to turn the decision-making over to them. Together you guys will carry on and bring a National Championship home." We all broke the meeting in good spirits.

The following Tuesday we lost our game 5-1. All the players saw playing time. Even though we lost, the subs were starting to contribute more to the team. This was a good time.

The next morning my attorney called to inform me that two FBI agents called her, asking for permission to talk to me. I asked her what this was about. She said she didn't know, but they did tell her that since I was now in the custody of the U.S. Attorney General, they had the permission of the U.S. Attorney's office and the Federal judge to talk to me. It was my decision. I said, "OK." The meeting was set for 10 a.m. in two days. I started to theorize: did they want me to be a snitch or some kind of informer? This was an interesting scenario.

The next day I went to the cemetery to visit my mother's and dad's graves. I stood by their graves thinking about my life and the past year. The line between the past and present was getting to feel very real. If we win the National Championship and a few girls get to go to college, was this the balance of my making bad choices and going to prison? Would I make that much of a difference by not being their coach for the rest of the season? All that money spent sponsoring this team, money that I used by not paying my sport shop bills. As I stood by the graves, I really believed those young softball players devoted their time, energy and spirit to achieve whatever goals awaited them at the finish line. I really believed the sport shop money had only provided the uniforms the girls were wearing. Their efforts were the real reason for their softball success and what lay ahead!! I only hoped their achievements were not marred by my behavior. I left the cemetery after a good hour of conscience-searching. The next day we all shared a long, intense practice. I worked the team hard. That night I pondered the next day's meeting with the FBI.

The next morning I traveled downtown to the FBI building. My lawyer was waiting. We both sat in the lobby wondering and curious. In came two well-dressed, polyester-suited guys, politely flashing their ID and thanking us for showing up. They led the way to the elevator, two flights up. From there we were escorted into a conference room. One of the agents spoke. This meeting was not about my crime or prison term. They were very much interested in me and what my plans were after my release. At that point, both agents asked if I would object to my attorney being excused from this meeting. No legal or incriminating questions would be discussed. Both agents left the conference room so that my lawyer and I could discuss their request. My lawyer offered to wait in the outer hall if I needed her. I told her that it was okay to leave – I'd be okay. She left and the two agents and I conducted about a two-hour meeting. I cannot reveal the results of this meeting; this closed-door meeting was a little puzzling and would result in a new factor in my life. I went to bed that night carrying the weight of my 230 lb. body in my head. I cannot and will not discuss this meeting or any results of this meeting again.

The next morning it was back to softball, and we had a game to play. The team looked and felt happy. We lost the game 7-2, but everyone played. The team didn't feel down. The softball team really gave me a relief of the mental strains; it was like a tonic, restoring my energy for what was ahead of me.

The following day, I kept myself busy with a lot of personal errands, seeing friends, breakfast at the coffee shop. While at the coffee shop, questions were asked by my friends: "Have you heard where the government is sending you and when?" "No news is good news," I answered. It was like waiting for that bus ride that was sure to come, but not knowing when. You wait and you think. You try to think about simple charms and pleasures and you have to retreat from any plans you might want to think about. I just wanted my report notice to arrive and get it all over with. By now, I was eager to report.

I went home that afternoon to check my mailbox – nothing. But I did have a message from one of my coaches. The coaches wanted to have a coffee shop meeting with me that night. An unusual request and a first, for my coaches to be calling a meeting with me. There was no practice or game that night, so the coaches and I met at the coffee shop. My first coach suggested that I call collect three times a week to the home of the parents of one of the players. This player's dad had a conference call system set up in his basement. The parents agreed that it would be a good idea to stay in close contact with the team. Of course, the players also would be present at these phone calls. I said it was a good idea, but I felt embarrassed about calling collect from a Federal prison. The coaches were concerned; some of the players were feeling less confident about themselves with my being away. They were having some intimidating thoughts about the National Tournament. One of the coaches expressed his feelings about his ability to take control of the team and to keep the winning tempo of this team claimed by my efforts and direction. The other coach added that none of the coaches had any national tournament experience, but they wanted to try, and they knew they had a challenging job ahead.

I looked at the coaches and the parent who was our scorekeeper and smiled. I said, "Thank you for the compliment. You have been very loyal to me and the team. Together, our fame or success will be a great test of character. Sometimes you find or lose yourself as a result of it – especially in the situation I created for us. But in the end, failures will be erased and success will be claimed. I will always treasure my memories of you and this softball team. This will be my weapon to face the other side of my life. You have a spirited and talented bunch of young girls to take with you to the National Tournament. They will be your weapons to carry you through tournament. So enough of any hesitations of the challenges ahead for you. These girls deserve the best from you. The collect phone calls from me to the parents' house is a good idea. We can keep in touch and monitor things together. "

After several cups of coffee until closing time, we all left. I went for a long drive around town, passing the old sport shop and the softball fields. I had a lot of thoughts to address. I had to gauge my worth and future contribution to this team. My itch for this team's success was allowing new energy in me. "No matter where I am, the illusion is the same. These girls are winners. Winning or losing softball games was only the vehicle they rode on to achieve goals and visions that were once vacant in their lives." I was getting tired of driving. Off to my apartment and to bed. Tomorrow was another day of softball practice.

# TIME TO GO

I slept in late the next morning. I just felt tired. I found myself opening the front door and sticking my hand into the mailbox. I pulled out one piece of mail. The return address read "U.S. Bureau of Prisons." This was it. I sat down and stared at the letter for about five minutes and started to open it slowly. There was no greeting. It just said that I had until 12:00 noon the next Monday to report to the Federal Prison Camp in Duluth, Minnesota. It also listed the items I was allowed to take with me:

One cap, no lettering on it
One t-shirt, no lettering
One sweatshirt, no lettering
One pair shoes – tennis shoes
One pair sweat pants, no lettering

All these items were to be of one solid color, except for the shoes.

The prison camp would only supply water and soap. All other toiletries had to be purchased through the commissary. No cash was allowed in your possession.

You had to purchase tokens for the laundry room service through the commissary.

It was all sinking in now. The time had come. I called my coaches to meet me early at the practice field. When I arrived at the softball field, I noticed a sign by the players' bench. I walked up to it. I just grinned. It was one of those prison signs. It read: PRISON PROPERTY, ONLY AUTHORIZED PERSONNEL. I guess the hecklers were still out there. When the other coaches arrived, I informed them not to remove the sign. "We will practice around and through it."

The players were now arriving and I informed the team of the sign and said, "This doesn't bother me, and it should not distract you from what we have to do. So let's practice."

All the players placed their softball gear on the other bench and just avoided the sign. We had a very good practice. Spirits were high, but I sensed a certain aggressive attitude about the players – like they were ready to beat any team. They appeared ready to vent some stress – maybe it was the sign. After practice almost every player walked past the sign and spit on it. They were ready to take it out on somebody.

The coaches and I went to the coffee shop, as usual. I showed them the "report to prison" letter. We talked about it. I told them I would take my favorite sweat jacket - my gray zip-down hooded one. I would also take my team hat, but I would have to remove the letter "A" on the hat. The hat had to be plain. One coach offered to have his wife remove the embroidered "A" from my hat. We talked about the next 3 months of the season. It was a quiet meeting, sort of sad. We now knew that there was a date – next Monday. My coaches asked me if I needed any help with preparing for Monday. They even wanted to drive me to Duluth. I told them that I was going to ask my oldest daughter and her boyfriend to drive me. I asked my coaches to focus on the team with complete attention to our goals: the players, especially the players armed for college, and the National Tournament. I said, "We have three games this week and we must keep feeding the team's appetite for winning and improving."

The following day was a day off for the team. I needed this day to pull myself together. I was walking around confidently, but I was walking with a silent fear. I called my oldest daughter that night and asked her to meet me the next night at our favorite coffee shop. The next day I made arrangements with the utility companies to disconnect my services that following Tuesday. I also had my mail forwarded to my oldest daughter's house.

Early evening came, and my daughter and I enjoyed supper at the coffee shop. I asked my daughter if she would drive me to Duluth on Sunday morning. I also wanted her to have her boyfriend with us. This was a 12-hour trip into the Upper Peninsula of Michigan and across the U.P. to Duluth. The return trip was not one for a young lady to take by herself. We discussed leaving at 8:00 a.m. on Sunday and spending the night outside the City of Duluth. I also told her to have the furniture in my apartment distributed equally among her and her sister and brother. I asked her to store my other personal belongings at her place. We both shed a few tears. I felt helpless. I had no options, and she knew that. I asked her not to visit me. I told her that I would also ask that my other daughter and son not visit. We talked about keeping in touch by mail and remembering the good things we shared together. I said, "It won't be long before this is all over and I'll be back." She told me that she and her sister and brother would be at our softball game.

I followed her home and then took another ride past the sport shop. The following morning I woke early and started sorting out some personal items for my daughter to store. Her auto insurance company provided us with directions to Duluth. I looked over these directions and routes. I called and made reservations for two rooms Sunday night outside of Duluth. It was a nice hotel facing Lake Superior.

My coaches wanted to pick me up for the game. We left a little early to discuss the line-up. I asked the coaches to make out the line-up card. I told them to trust their instincts; it was time for them to march to the finish line. I said, "You have a talented bunch of young ladies armed with energy and spirit. Enjoy the ride."

The players started showing up. They were ready. They knew this was my last game with them, and they played like it was for the National Championship. We won, 11-0. There were more than the usual parents and friends at this game.

After the game I called a team meeting. Most of the parents and friends stayed. Some of the parents thanked me for helping their daughters become better softball players and for giving them the tools and the will to pursue college. It was hard to hold back a tear pushing my eyelid. I told the parents and friends that it had been an enjoyable privilege for me to be a part of all of this, and asked everyone to continue to support these girls and their goals. I then asked the parents and friends to allow me a few minutes alone with my team. I took the team a few yards into the outfield. We all relaxed. I paused for about two minutes and looked at everyone individually.

I said, "Over a year ago people were laughing at you while you were walking off a softball field. Now, these people are sending their young daughters to you for your autograph. Over a year ago, you came to my sport shop, asking me to coach you. I agreed, however, with certain conditions – huge emphasis on loyalty, sacrifices and hard work were some of my demands. I offered no shortcuts, and told you that you must touch all bases. I stand witness to your results. Here we are, poised for the National Championship. You are ready and you deserve it. It makes no difference who writes out the line-up now. I want to thank you for believing in me.    Shortly I will be leaving, but I'm not leaving empty-handed. I'm taking your laughter and smiles from your wins and losses. These will be my companions."

The next day was Saturday. I wanted to have an early practice at 2:00 p.m., because I had some things to do before Sunday morning. My coaching staff and I met at the coffee shop for our last meeting together. I explained to them that if we won the National Tournament, the Tournament Committee would award 20 individual trophies to the players, and two extra trophies for the coaches. Since the tournament allowed only 20 players on the playing roster and we had 22 players, I asked them to list the other two players as Scorekeeper and Batgirl. That would allow us to have all 22 players in full uniform on the players' bench.

I said, "Should we win – and we will win – give the 22 trophies to the players. Also, keep playing everyone at all games until three weeks prior to the tournament in August. Play our best players more and push them hard. They have the stamina and the willpower to prevail, whatever they encounter. Keep this team intact to the road map we all have laid out together.

"Now, I want to discuss tomorrow's work out. We want to conduct a three-hour practice. We will start at 2 p.m. and no one leaves until practice has ended at 5 p.m. During this practice there will be no good-byes said. At some point during the practice I will just gradually make my way to my car and drive away. Keep the players focused on the practice. We have a game plan to stay in touch. I will call on Tuesday and Thursday nights."
We all paused for a minute, and I hugged my coaches. We left the coffee shop in separate cars and drove off. I

went back to my apartment and wrote out some game situation instructions for my coaches.

I had a Saturday morning breakfast planned with my three kids. At breakfast I reminded my kids not to drive to Duluth to see me. I also apologized to them for any embarrassing gossip relating to my prison sentence. I told them that I loved them. We hugged and none of us could hold back any tears. This was not the time to hold back anything. I discussed the trip Sunday morning to Duluth. I gave my oldest daughter money to gas up her car. We planned on leaving at 7:30 Sunday morning.

I had a short stop to make at a florist. I instructed the florist to deliver 22 yellow roses to the softball field, where my team was to be practicing softball, at exactly 4:30 p.m. I asked the florist to read each player's name while handing her a yellow rose. The florist knew about our team and agreed to do what I had asked, but would not accept my money for the flowers and service. She said that her 11-year old daughter had watched our team practice, and was saving up enough money to purchase a softball glove and shoes to someday try out for our team.

I thanked the florist and went off to the hair salon for a trim. My stomach was in knots; time was getting short. It was almost time for our 2 p.m. practice.

I went home to change into my coaching shorts. It was a warm day, and I wanted to arrive a little early for practice. I wanted to remember our practice field and the mirrored image of my players. However, I wasn't the only one to arrive early. All 22 players in full uniform, clean shoes and all, were warming up, doing their stretch-out exercises and playing catch. They looked gorgeous. A coach isn't supposed to feel empty and at a loss for words; a coach is supposed to demonstrate strength. This was not easy. The players, my coaches and I had bonded.

As I approached the players' bench, I instructed my team to meet at home plate. It was silent, and I just looked at everyone's face, then yelled, "Let's practice!"

I let the coaches start the practice, and then I motioned for them to meet with me. We discussed the season and went over the batting line-up for the upcoming games. We had a very fast runner that we wanted to keep as our lead-off hitter. Our next batter was also a fast runner who liked to slash out at the ball. She could hit behind the runners. With our first two hitters having good speed and being good contact hitters, we weren't involved in too many double plays. Our third and fourth hitters could hit the ball hard. We also scored runs early in the game. Scoring early gave us momentum. We really had no weak hitters; everyone made good contact with the ball. I looked at my coaches and said, "Just do it."

The coaches turned their attention back to conducting practice. I stood by the bench and watched. After a while I slowly started drifting toward the parking lot, then drove off and didn't look back. I went to my apartment and emptied my car. Then I started packing for the morning drive to Duluth. I sorted out things at the apartment and made a list of things for my kids to take and share. I only had one duffle bag to pack. While I was packing my sweatshirt, I noticed some writing on the inside of the shirt. The players had signed their names on the inside. It was nice, but puzzling. I couldn't remember when the team had had access to my sweatshirt. The next day would be a long ride, so I went to bed early.

# THE LONG RIDE

Morning came, and my daughter and her boyfriend showed up promptly as planned at 7:30 a.m. We started out on I-75 North. Since we were in no hurry, we stopped outside Saginaw for breakfast. We didn't talk about the place I was reporting to. We mostly talked about the plans my daughter and her boyfriend had made. He said he loved my daughter and wanted to marry her. My daughter said that maybe this was not the time to discuss it. I said, "Where I'm going is not important; your life and happiness *is* important to me." So, for the next six hours, they both went on and on about when they had met and the things they did together. I was happy for them and it took away some other thoughts about my destination.

We were approaching the beautiful Mackinac Bridge. We crossed over into the Upper Peninsula of Michigan and started our journey on Highway 2 toward Wisconsin. We stopped for lunch in a small village near a lumber mill. It was a strange ride; traffic was light and the scenery was plentiful. Sometimes we would leave Michigan, enter Wisconsin, and re-enter Michigan. Eleven hours into the trip, we entered Minnesota. We stopped outside Duluth at the motel where I had made reservations. It faced Lake Superior, and at the rear of the motel was a small beach. We checked in and after dinner, we were all tired. We agreed to meet for breakfast at 10 a.m.

That night I lay in bed, deep in thought. I was looking for my childhood conditioning to face another side of my life.

When morning finally came, we had breakfast, but not too much was said. I reminded my daughter to have a safe trip back home. We had an hour to check out of our rooms. I wanted to walk by the water, alone. I told my daughter that I would meet them in the motel lobby in about a half hour. I walked along the edge of Lake Superior and sat down on the beach. After about ten minutes, I tipped my face to the sun and sucked in the clean air from the lake. It was a cool morning and I wore my sweatshirt with all the players' names written inside. This was not a time for tears, but they came anyway. My basic skills needed to come into play here.

I walked away from the cool lake breeze, and as I approached the entrance to the hotel lobby, my daughter and her boyfriend approached. They had paid the hotel bill and now handed me the car keys. Before we got into the car, I hugged my daughter and held her. It was time to take that ten-minute ride to the prison's front gate.

I drove slowly into the prison compound, stopped at the guardrail and identified myself. I was told to drive around to the Control Center and take a seat in the lobby.

We didn't see any armed guards around. There were inmates walking around. We saw a few small white cars driving slowly, observing everyone. I guessed these were the guards.

I stopped at the entrance to the Control Center. I was the only one allowed to get out of the car. My daughter scooted over on the driver's side and gave me a kiss. I watched them drive away. She kept looking back, waving her hand out of the window.

# THE LONG STAY

I went into the lobby with the personal things that I was allowed to bring. In about ten minutes, a guard came up to me and escorted me to another room. Another guard was there. They both examined the personal clothing I had brought in. I was fingerprinted and a photo was taken of me. I was then taken to another room where I was asked to strip off all of my clothes. My clothing was placed in a basket, to be given back to me upon my release. The extra clothes that I had brought with me were to be my temporary clothing during orientation.

They gave me a map of the compound and instructed me to proceed to Building B. I was assigned an upper bunk bed in a room with three other bunk beds. This would be my home for the next year. A guard issued me a booklet of prison rules. In the next five days, I would be going through orientation. They would inform me of times and places of the orientation, but in between these times, I was free to walk around the compound or go to the gym. I had to sign a sheet describing the time and place that I would be at all times.

As 4 p.m. approached, inmates started coming from all over, returning to their assigned buildings. I was told that they were coming back from their jobs; that every inmate had to work while in prison – no exceptions. If you were caught in your bunk bed during working hours, you needed to have a doctor's written order from the infirmary. I was by my bunk bed when three other inmates came in. They introduced themselves. They explained to me that at 4:30 p.m. you had to be standing up beside your bed. A guard would come around and take a head count. Once they finished the head count (it took about 20 minutes), you would hear over the P.A. system, "All clear." You then were free to go to chow. This was suppertime – 5 to 6:30 p.m. The kitchen closed promptly at 6:30 p.m. After supper, you were free to walk the compound, go to the library, the gym, or sign up for a collect phone call that lasted 15 minutes.

The Phone Center was in the Recreational Building, which also housed the TV room, three pool tables and a vending machine that was operated by tokens. I was told that at 8:45 p.m. a bell would sound, giving us 15 minutes to be back at our bedside for another head count. This head count was done while the guard had your picture in his hand. After this picture head count was concluded and cleared, you were free to take a shower, write letters or watch TV.

There was a non-smoking TV room on the second level and a smoking TV room on the first level. The TV room was shut down at 11 p.m., Monday through Thursday, and 1 a.m. Friday through Sunday. No one had to work on Saturday or Sunday.

Most of the advice and information about the prison was offered to me by a guy named Gabby. I guess he liked to talk. He bunked two doors down the hall. No one talked about what crime they had committed, and no one asked about my crime. You had to be inside your own bunk bed room at 12, midnight. The guards were called "hacks" among the inmates, but when you spoke to a guard, it was "sir" or "ma'am," make no mistake about that.

That first night, time went by fast; I guess because I was being a good listener and I wanted to be quickly educated about prison life. As I lay in bed, I couldn't believe where I was. As midnight approached, it became very quiet. Radios were not allowed. You could purchase a radio from the commissary; however, you also had to purchase a headset.

At about 6 a.m. you could hear inmates waking up and making their way to the bathrooms and shower areas, which were halfway down the hall. A couple of my roommates showed me how to fix my bed, hospital style, nothing to be left out. Everyone had his own small cabinet.

Breakfast was served in the kitchen building from 6:30 to 7:30 a.m. Everyone had to report to his job by 7:45 a.m. for a head count by the work supervisor. After breakfast, I returned to my bunk and signed out to the baseball diamond area. For a small moment, this became a connection to the outside world. I sat in the bleachers and just thought about my softball team. I walked around the outfield for about two hours, just circling the field, thinking of my softball team practicing. I needed to weather the changes I would be facing. I took a walk to the church. (This prison had tennis courts, a gym, an education center, a baseball diamond, and a post office. Everything here was run by inmates.) I went inside the church and sat down in the pew. Here I was in church, saying a few prayers. Isn't it always when you're down in life and trying to restore your self-esteem, that you turn to God? Fame or success is a great test of character. You try to erase your failures and claim a sense of self-acceptance.

I thought about everything that had happened leading up to this. I was really puzzled about the FBI. In one newspaper article describing my criminal activity leading to my arrest, the FBI was quoted as saying that a local rival sport shop had tipped them off about my large purchases of sporting goods from vendors, and my inability to pay for the purchases. However, in the FBI's investigation notes submitted to the U.S. Attorney's office for my indictment, it said that the UPS driver became suspicious and informed the FBI. I don't believe either of the stories. There is one thing you have in prison – plenty of time to think through everything that led up to it all.

I walked back to the bunk area and checked the notice board in the hall. I was scheduled for orientation the next day at 2 p.m. Four o'clock was approaching, and inmates were starting to flock toward their buildings and bunk areas for the head count. My roommates came in tired. No one talks too much. The hack (guard) came around, looked at us, marked his chart and swiftly walked away to the Control Center. Twenty-five minutes later the all-clear sound came from the P.A.

There were four bunk buildings. Each building was called by its turn to proceed to chow. Actually, the food wasn't that bad. After supper, I started to walk around the compound. I was joined by three other inmates; one was the guy they called Gabby – he sure liked to talk. We walked and we talked. We walked and we talked. Mostly small talk. Gabby told us he was in for drugs, serving his fourth year and two to go before release. He said he hadn't seen his daughter in four years, although his wife visited him once a month. He also was from Michigan. We kept walking. It was almost June, but the cool air from Lake Superior felt like October. Everyone offered their version of the orderly arrangement of the prison rules. I guessed I'd find out everything at 2 p.m. the next day.

After spending about two hours in the TV room, I took my nightly shower and went to bed. I just lay there. "Am I really here?" My thoughts seemed to alternate between being scared and having acceptance. It feels like you have a secret disgrace that will occupy your heart forever.

I woke up around 6 the next morning. The first voice I heard was Gabby down the hall, talking it up. "706 days to go," as his voice trailed off to the chow hall. After breakfast that morning, I'd decided to go to the gym to check out the weight room. I'm not a big fan of pumping iron; it tightens your muscles too much. You can't throw a baseball with tight muscles. I tossed a few basketballs and jogged around the gym. I'm not much of a breakfast person, but my gym visit gave me an appetite for a good lunch.

After lunch I walked around the baseball field until my 2 p.m. orientation. There were 16 new inmates in the room. Before too long a tall guy dressed in a polyester suit walked in and introduced himself as the Warden. He handed out a small booklet and said, "Read it, and when you're done, read it again. Don't lose it. Without it you'll be lost in here." He pointed toward the main entrance of the prison and said, "There are no fences here. This is a Level One security prison. If you want to walk out of here, go ahead. We're not going to chase you, but when the U.S. Marshals catch up with you, you'll do your time double, behind the walls of a Level Five prison.

"When you leave this meeting, you will proceed to the clothing building. They will issue you two pairs of pants, two shirts, two pairs of socks and one pair of safety shoes. All the same color. You are required to wear this clothing from 6:30 a.m. until 4:30 p.m. After the

4 p.m. head count, you may wear the clothing you brought in with you, described in your report notice.

"Everyone works. You will be assigned a job. We are community here. We have rules. You are in a Federal prison and you are here for a reason – a reason that you alone demonstrated. You will be given a psychological test. You will be examined by a doctor and a dentist. You will be assigned to a counselor who will meet with you periodically. You will be assigned an inmate number and post office box number for your mail. All incoming mail will be opened and checked for contraband.

"While you work, everyone starts at nine cents an hour. These funds are applied to your commissary account. You must purchase tokens for the laundry machines and vending machines. You are allowed 15-minute collect phone calls that you must sign up for in advance. We also listen and monitor your phone calls. Read your booklet. All this information and more is in this booklet. Any inmate exercising any sexual act with another inmate will be charged with a crime and punished accordingly. You are here because you brought yourself here, and only you can bring yourself out."

No one spoke except the Warden. He thanked us for our attention and left. He gave us our wake-up call.

After the meeting, I went back to my bunk and wrote a letter to my coaches, giving them my mailing address. After supper, I went to the Recreation Center to sign up for a Thursday night phone call to my coaches. At about 8:30 that night after the head count, I took my evening shower and lay in bed thinking. My thoughts became instincts. I lay in bed trying to listen to my instincts. I was re-living the past 16 months in thoughts. If I had the chance to do it all over again, would I do it? I was weighing the bad against the good. How else would these young girls have had the opportunity to play on a first-class softball program, visiting colleges? Did we buy the opportunity for them? Am I paying the price for all of this now? One thing was certain: the hard work and the funds provided an opportunity that had not existed before, and the results were showing. Am I a hero? No. What I did was wrong, but if it made a difference in some young girls' lives, then so be it. I didn't want the girls to know that the money used to further their opportunity was compromised by my present situation. It's a short time for me in here. It's a longer time for them to enjoy a better future. I could think and play the results over and over again. I had no regrets. Tomorrow was another day for me to pass the time away.

The next morning after breakfast I walked over to the baseball field. I walked around the field several times. After a couple of hours, I went back to my bunk area. I checked the bulletin board. I was assigned to mechanical services. My job was to re-paint buildings with four other painters. I was to report to work at 7:30 a.m. the next day for a check-in.

That night at dinnertime, I sat next to Gabby. I told him I was assigned to do painting. Gabby always referred to me as "short time" because I was only there for eight months. After dinner the four of us continued to walk around the compound. Gabby talked, we listened. It was always the same routine.

The next morning I reported for work. That morning I was assigned to paint some roof vents. An inmate would drive a truck with ladders and take me to the building I was to work on. So, my paintbrush and I became close friends.

I was looking forward to my first phone call that evening. I heard a voice that I had missed. I held back a tear or two. It was a conference call to my coach. I could hear the team in the background, "We miss you and we're practicing hard. We're going to win the Nationals." I told the coaches and the team my thoughts were with them. I told them that they were my weapons to get me through this. The 15 minutes came and went so fast and another tear came with the hang-up. I saw Gabby in the doorway. We walked around the compound talking until it was time for our head count back at the bunk area. Bedtime came and I slept better.

The next day I went about painting roof vents. After work I went to the post office building. What a surprise – about 12 letters and an envelope with a picture of our team! We were allowed to have three pictures tacked up on the wall by our bed. I proudly hung the team picture. The team looked so neat in their uniforms.

That night after our usual walk around the compound, Gabby and another guy came by my bunk. They gave special attention to the softball team's picture. They knew I was a coach and that this was my team. Gabby especially stared at the picture for a few minutes. He then asked me about one of the players in the picture. He wanted to know her name. I paused and told him a different name than that of the player. I didn't know his reason for asking and I didn't want any of my softball players' names disclosed to any of these inmates. Gabby just nodded his head and went to the TV room. The rest of the evening I kept busy reading all of my letters. All of the letters were opened prior to being placed in my mailbox, for prison inspection for contraband. I felt even better after reading the letters. I felt like I was still with the team.

After tucking away my letters, I took my nightly shower. When you lie in bed, you think and you think. This prison has a gym, a softball field, a library, an education center, a church and a recreation building. But make no mistake – this was prison. You were told how to dress, when to sleep, eat, work, get your mail, and where to be at certain times. There was no personal contact with the outside. You were confined to about 120 acres, and everyone worked 5 days a week for nine cents an hour. You invented thoughts and tortured yourself with ideas. The "feeling sorry for yourself" trap didn't work here. There were no role models for us. You staked out your own emotional territory every day. In the short time I'd been there I seemed to be out-maneuvered by professional liars who became rich and powerful with loopholes they'd created for themselves. I saw complainers, whiners and lazy ex-businessmen who talked about their stock options, new cars, planes, boats and lastly, their families. All this had turned against them. They were here. No one ever admits it, though. They continue to believe it's a comfort theory, rather than everyday reality. I was tired. It was another night of lonely sleep.

The next few weeks were all the same routine. The boosts to my spirit were the letters from my players and the phone calls to my coaches. The phone calls were special because I could hear my players in the background. I let them know that their voices and letters kept my spirits high. For a moment I could be happy again. For a moment I could hear their voices. For a moment I was their coach again. For another night, I could sleep easy again.

After work the next day, I needed to write a serious letter to the coaches and the team. Time was getting close to the National Tournament. In past conversations with the coaches, they had told me that some of the players were getting bored and sometimes dragging themselves during ballgames. There could not be a letdown. Even some parents questioned the spirit of the team, and there were even thoughts of "why go the National Tournament?" I received a letter from one parent saying that at times the coaches seemed to lose control of the team. I had been worried about something like that happening.

Prison has a way of separating you from your other life. I wasn't going to let prison derail these girls from their visions and goals. Prison was not going to separate us from the spirit and bond we shared. The next day while I was working, I kept thinking about how to keep the team's spirit together and to keep them focused on all we had worked for over the past 16 months. That night I walked around the compound by myself. I stayed away from Gabby. I needed the time alone. I signed up for my usual phone call to the coaches and the team for the next night. After that I went back to my bunk area.

That night in bed I did a lot of thinking. There were a lot of lives entangled in the landscape of softball, colleges, and my situation. The texture of relationships in the prison was tolerance and respecting other inmates. Inmates extended loyalty to each other, not to the prison staff. Those who abided by the inmates' rules got respect. The agenda was to try to listen to the few real people and not the performers. This was the first step toward learning about prison life. In the three months I'd been there, I'd come to understand that no personal success could erase the stigma of being an ex-con. I think the real test for me was to be self-correcting. To do this, I had to be open and truthful about myself. The softball team and I together took us to a new level of life. We were 700 miles apart physically, but mentally that bond between us took away those miles. I was able to fall asleep with a smile.

# <u>Creating A Plan</u>

Morning came, Gabby came, and off to breakfast we went. I asked Gabby to walk with me that evening around the compound. There was something I wanted to ask him.

After work that day I made that happy stroll to the mailroom. As usual, several letters arrived from my players, coaches and some parents. I always took my letters to my bunk area to read them in private. This was my silent time for myself. Gabby knew it, too. If he came by to talk and saw me reading, he would just walk on by.

That evening after supper, Gabby and I went for our hour-long walk around the compound. I asked Gabby if he were to sign up for a 15-minute phone call, would he be willing to pass it to me? This way I could have 30 minutes to talk to my team and coaches. He would sign up for the 15 minutes following my 15 minutes. Gabby said in his four years of being there, he couldn't remember this happening, but he liked the idea and we both agreed to try it. Gabby knew that I was involved with a world-class softball team, and he told me that he had a young daughter playing somewhere in Michigan. We both went to the Recreation Center to sign up. After we signed up, we talked to the "hack" in charge of the phone area. (There were 15 phones.) This guard was the softball coordinator for the main men's softball team that represented Duluth Federal Prison in a league made up of eight teams. Seven teams from Duluth and the 8th team, the prison team, played all of their scheduled games on the prison grounds. This guard, they said, was respected for being fair. He asked me why I needed 30 minutes. I explained the girls' softball team and the National Tournament date approaching. He said that Gabby needed to understand that once he forfeited his phone call for that day, he had no phone privileges for the rest of the night. Gabby happily agreed. It was all set. I had 30 minutes for the next night. I thanked Gabby, and we walked around some more and talked. While we were walking that night, I had an idea. When I called the team the next night, I was going to run the idea by my coaches. I felt good! Another night, another smile to fall asleep to.

The next day, I was scheduled to paint the inside of a guard's house, just outside the gate. This guard had been transferred and a new guard would be coming soon. They had given me four days to finish painting the interior of this house. It had three small bedrooms, two baths, and a normal size kitchen and living room. This was good – four days working by myself. Time to think and work on an idea I had. After supper Gabby and I went to the Recreation Center to claim our phone time. I had a lot to say to my team and to the coaches. It was my turn to walk to phone #7. I placed my collect call to the coach's house. I was on speaker phone. I said, "Hello team!" About 24 or so voices answered, "Hi coach, we miss you!" I asked if all the players were present, and the coach said they were. I thanked both coaches for working so hard at keeping the team together and for taking my call. I said, "I have about 28 minutes left to visit with you. The first part of my visit with you concerns the coaches. I would like you to contact Bell South in Tullahoma, Tennessee, to have a phone with a private number installed at the concession stand near Diamond #1 One. Order 100 feet of phone cord. All semi-final games and the championship game will be played on Diamond #1 One. I have written a letter to the Tournament Director asking permission for this. He understands our situation and I have his favorable reply in writing. I am sending you a copy of this reply. Make sure the phone is in place and working by Friday morning the weekend of the Tournament. It's going to cost around $200.00. Call my oldest daughter – she will supply you with the funds."

Many voices on the other end of this phone conversation replied, "That won't be necessary. We'll take care of everything."

I told my team that I knew they would be in the finals, playing on Diamond #1 One. "I will try to secure enough phone time to help you through the tournament by talking to the coaches during the games." Then I said, "OK team, now it's time to talk about us. Together we won games, together we lost games, together we were happy, together we were sad. But together, we never quit. And nobody is quitting. We have nine days to work together before Nationals. You must mentally maintain the same loyalty and dedication to each other that you have demonstrated for the past 16 months. You owe each other this. You will remember this National Tournament for the rest of your life. Your fans and friends will also remember this with you. I probably won't be talking to you again until we meet again on Diamond #1 in the finals. My thoughts and feelings will be with you every inning of the Tournament. Have fun and get the job done! You're ready!"

I hung up the phone. I think I had about four minutes left, but I couldn't talk anymore. I couldn't hold back the tears that wanted to just run out. I left the phone area and Gabby followed me. He knew I needed to find my composure. So, we walked a silent ½ mile and I looked at Gabby and thanked him for his phone time. Gabby handed me the hooded sweatshirt that I had left on the phone chair. He noticed the names signed on the inside of the shirt and asked if these names were the names of my softball team. I replied, "Yes." Then Gabby said, "After our walk and the head count, can I look at your team picture again?" I said, "Sure." I didn't ask him why and I didn't think too much about it. That evening he came to my bunk area. He walked over to the team picture tacked on the wall by my bed. He pointed to a player in the picture and said, "She's my daughter." He told me her name and pointed to the signed names on the inside of my shirt. What are the odds of this happening? We talked some and agreed to talk again at tomorrow night's walk.

# THE VISIT

After work the next day, I hurriedly went to the mailroom. Mail was the highlight of my day. There were always letters from my kids, my players, and today, a letter from one of my coaches. It was a welcome surprise! He was flying in to see me the following Sunday! He wanted to discuss the National Tournament. He had received all the material from the Tournament, including the schedule. Our first game was the following Friday night, against a team from Washington, PA. My coach appeared nervous in his letter.

My next step was to go to my counselor and add my coach's name to the inmate visiting list; no one can visit an inmate without the inmate's consent. After supper Gabby and I went to the softball diamond to watch the inmates play a league game against a team from Duluth. While watching the game, Gabby really pumped me about his daughter being on my team and about preparations for the trip to Tennessee for the tournament. Gabby wanted to know if his daughter was a regular player on the team. He asked about her attitude while playing softball. His wife had told him that their daughter was playing on a local softball team, but this was too awesome! He talked and he talked. He acted like an expectant father, waiting in a hospital delivery room. I was very honest with him. I told him that his daughter was very much an integral part of the team. She had good team spirit, had good speed on the bases, and was given a lot of playing time. She was very respectful of the coaching staff and her teammates.

We both enjoyed watching the prison team play their league game. Gabby said that some of the guys on the team had been playing together for some years. The prison team looked fair. They needed work on fundamentals, and on the in-between stuff, in addition to the hitting and running. The Recreation Director was their coach. It was a job that the Director didn't really want, but it was assigned to him by the Warden. It's one thing to encourage a bunch of inmates during a softball game, and still another to display strong discipline to the same inmates in the yard of the compound.

Gabby and I went for our nightly walk. He asked several questions about the girls' tournament. I told Gabby that the opening ceremony of the Girls' National Softball Tournament was a beautiful sight. The teams from each state are announced, and the player representing her state runs to the outfield section of the infield, holding her state flag. Then a band plays the National Anthem. It is a very colorful sight. During this part of the ceremony, an award is presented to the best-uniformed team. While the players compete in the tournament, committees choose twelve all-star players, a tournament queen, and an award is given to the team displaying the best sportsmanship. Large trophies are presented to the championship team, the runner-up team, and the third place finishers, and individual trophies are awarded to each player on the championship team and runner-up team.

That night we walked until almost head count time. Even after the nightly head count, Gabby came to our bunk area. Again, he looked at the team picture near my bedside. Gabby said that he hadn't seen his daughter in years, but he knew she was in the 10th grade.

The next day was Saturday. Inmates don't work on Saturdays or Sundays. I needed to prepare for my coach's visit on Sunday. There was so much to discuss about the phone set-up and the tournament. This was going to be my first visit from the outside, and probably my last until my release. Saturday morning after breakfast, I went for a walk by the softball field. I wanted to be by myself. I sat in the bleachers and stood at the infield. How many times had I pictured myself drilling my players on a ball field – yelling out instructions and correcting their bad softball habits? I missed the outside world. In prison you are nobody; there is no pleasure and you feel ignored. It's like being absorbed in endless punishment. That was the society of the inmates in that compound. You had to be officially and socially hurt and punished. Then everything was supposed to be all right again. Justice would have been served. It was therapeutic in some instances; restraining in some ways. I guess this is society's machinery at work again. It's expensive, it's stupid. Some of these inmates should have been sent to a doctor instead of a prison. I got up and walked around the outfield until lunch. After lunch, I went to the mailroom and opened my mailbox. As usual, some letters. These letters seem to be a beacon from the world I left behind.

I went back to the softball bleachers to read my letters. I was half way through my reading when the prison softball team arrived for practice. I began making my way back to my bunk area, but the hack stopped me and asked me to stay awhile and watch practice. This was the same guard who was in charge of the regulated phone system. I was thinking that I needed to be on the good side of this hack, but I didn't want to appear to suck up to him, or I'd be an outcast with the other inmates. I casually walked back to the bleachers. I watched their practice, but I was also doing some letter-reading, so that it wouldn't seem like I was doing any favors or sucking up to the guard. I watched and read for about an hour, then left for my room. I wanted to work on an agenda for the next day, when the coach was flying in to see me. I was getting nervous and feeling ashamed.

I heard loud voices. It was Gabby and he was looking happy and proud. The inmate with Gabby kept saying "whatever Gabby has been drinking, I want some."

Believe it or not, on the weekends, some inmates take grape juice, add a few ingredients, and heat it up. They drink it, and it makes them laugh and they seem to talk more. It helped them forget a little of being in prison. Gabby was telling everyone that his daughter played on a softball team that might win a national championship the following weekend.

The next weekend was Labor Day. The airfield next door was putting on an air show on Sunday. Most of the inmates would be in attendance. Gabby said that it was a yearly thing here, and a lot of the hacks watched it with their families. Gabby knew I was preparing some paperwork for my coach's visit the next day, so he and the fellow with him left.

I was writing and thinking about what to say the next day to my coach. I had an idea and I wanted to run it by him. I went to supper and then to find Gabby. I found him in the Recreation Center. He was getting ready to make a phone call – probably calling his wife and daughter and maybe talking about the softball tournament. I wondered if he was going to tell his family that his daughter's softball coach was keeping company with him in here.

I waited for Gabby. As he left the phone area, he seemed calm and relaxed. He looked at me and we left together for our nightly walk. Gabby said that he didn't want his wife and daughter to know that we knew each other in here, at least not until after the tournament. I told Gabby that was a smart idea – let's not upset the picture until after the tournament.

As we were walking, one of the white prison station wagons pulled up. The hack said that the Recreation Center guard wanted to see me. My stomach dropped to my knees. Gabby looked at me. He said, "You better go."

I walked back to the Recreation Center. I went directly to the guard's desk. He was busy assigning phone times to inmates. He said, "Have a seat." I waited for about 45 minutes. He motioned for me to approach his desk. He said, "You know we have four softball teams in the prison compound and one major team in the Duluth City League. These players could use a good softball clinic. Would you be interested in conducting this clinic?" He said, "We can't make you do this. It's strictly up to you, but I may recommend in writing to the Warden seven days of extra good time on your sentence release." My mind really started to work, especially since I had an idea pending about the softball tournament. The Recreation guard told me that he had read my complete file as well as all those letters written to the judge by players and friends. I answered that I would conduct the clinic and that I would need a few softball items in order to do it. He told me to put it in writing and he'd have it for me. We agreed to have the clinic on the Saturday after Labor Day weekend, because the air show was on Labor Day weekend.

I left and went to catch up with Gabby. I told him what took place with the Recreation hack. I told Gabby that I had to do it because I had a plan for Labor Day weekend to help coach my team. I asked Gabby to change our walk routine to walk a different route, because I wanted to talk about something important. I asked Gabby if he thought it would be possible to get enough inmates to sign up for phone time on Saturday and Sunday, from 9 a.m. to 9 p.m. Right away, Gabby caught on. He knew I had the coaches order a phone on Diamond #1. All of the semi-final games, as well as the championship game, would be played on that diamond. I could call collect and talk to the coach during the game and also talk to him about the games leading up to Diamond #1. The coach could relay information to my other coach at the other diamond. The softball diamonds are together in one complex. There are four diamonds adjoining one another, but the phone line extended from the concession stand to Diamond #1.

Gabby was excited. He started to get loud. I had to calm him. I told him that we still had to secure 36 other inmates to sign up for phone times 15 minutes apart on phone #7, which was in the corner of the aisle of phones. Gabby spoke very confidently and directly: "I will get the inmates. You do your thing – let's win this thing for the girls." Finally, Gabby was a part of this. He sensed it, and he was happy. His daughter was playing, and he could be 25 feet away from me talking on the phone while the team was playing. He knew I would be able to hear the cheers and the voices of the girls playing for the National Championship 1400 miles away.

I told Gabby to "slow down, you're walking too fast. I can't think." I said, "Gabby, you know even if you get the 36 inmates to participate in this, we still have to get by the Recreation guard." Gabby said, "Now I know why you agreed to do this softball clinic for the prison, especially a week after Labor Day weekend. We now have terrific leverage with the Recreation hack. The hack wants the clinic to be a success and we want the phone minutes tied up on Saturday and Sunday of Labor Day weekend." Gabby said that he had a lot of visiting to do beginning the next day. "People owe me favors in here and I'm calling in those favors. I'll get the phone time. You work the Recreation hack."

That night I couldn't sleep. I was thinking about the next day's visit from my coach. I had so much to discuss with him. The next morning, I shaved and went to breakfast. No sign of Gabby; he must have been recruiting inmates for phone sign-ups. I went for a walk, trying to relax my mind. About two hours passed, and finally my number was read on the P.A. system to report to the Visiting Center. I was nervous. I walked slowly toward the Visitors' Building. All inmates receiving visitors must walk through a rear entrance. There, we were "shook down" and our hats were removed. I signed in for my visit at the guard desk. I looked up across the room, and there he was – my coach. We hugged and looked at each other.

"You've lost some weight," he said. I told him that I had lost about 20 pounds. We hugged some more. He said, "Look! I have all this change for the vending machines. Let's have a soda pop." We sat down on the wooden bench. The coach said, "The team sends their love and wants you to know that they're ready!" He said that he had some pictures for me, but the guard took them and told him that I could pick them up the next day in the mailroom. We got right down to business. He said, "I'm scared. This national tournament is too big for us to comprehend." I looked into his eyes and stared: "Look!" I said. "This team will do it all for you. Just maintain a high level of confidence and verbal spirit. There is no crystal ball here that's going to talk you through this. The team will do the rest!"

He showed me the tournament papers and the double elimination bracket. We played Friday night against Washington, PA. I didn't know anything about that team. I said, "Don't be impatient. Let the first couple of innings play out. Let the girls get the feel for the situation. Their softball skills will come into play."

We talked about the opening ceremonies. My coach said that they had the state flag, and the team was prepped about the ceremonies. He said they were expecting about 25 cars to leave Michigan with parents and fans. Some of the fans and parents chipped in for the players' food. The coach also said he had the money I had given him earlier for the trip and that everything was fine financially.

He started to tell me that the players and some other people were concerned about me, but I stopped him before he could finish his sentence. "The objective here is the team," I said. "The time has come, and it's coming with energy and spirit fueled by months, weeks and hours of hard work. It's their place in time and it's going to happen. And you, you're the coach – look, feel and display confidence. The team needs to see this in you! And tell the other coach the same thing. Now, let's get down to the business of the phone. We are working on something that may allow me to talk to you from 6:00 p.m. to 8:45 p.m. on Friday night, and from 8:30 a.m. to 8:45 p.m. on Saturday and Sunday. The calls all will be collect. Try to get one of the parents to scout the team we would be playing next on Saturday. If you're not on Diamond #1 one, you still can take the calls from the concession stand."

After about four hours of talking and four soda pops to wash down our candy bars and chips, we had to say good-bye. My coach looked a lot better leaving than he had coming in. We hugged and I told him to "get the job done!"

I went through the rear hall and was strip-searched and released to the compound. I wanted to walk. I was so sad. Gabby said, "Well, maybe I can get a smile from your big nose. So far, I got 22 commitments for phone calls for you, and that's in the last nine hours." I thanked Gabby and we talked and we walked.

Back at our bunk area, Gabby wanted to look at the team picture again. He smiled. He said, "We're going to get those phone times. You get the Recreation hack to agree, then do your thing on the phone." Gabby got loud; he was pumped up. We both called it a night.

The next day was Wednesday – two days until Friday and the first game of the tournament. I went about my painting job. That afternoon I heard my inmate number announced over the P.A. system, telling me to report to the Control Center. I dropped my paintbrush and made my way over there. The guard at the desk told me to take a seat; that the Warden would see me shortly. After about five minutes, my counselor walked in. He greeted me and told me that the Warden wanted my file. He also told me that anytime an inmate is summoned by the Warden, the inmates' counselor also is summoned. As the desk guard directed us to the Warden's office, the knot in my stomach went down to my legs. We went into the Warden's office. The Warden was all bowtie and pinstripes surrounded by a jungle of plants. His baritone voice spoke with high authority.

"Good afternoon. I have two issues on my desk that we need to address. I have a list of supplies and equipment you have requested for our softball clinic. I have approved these items." The Warden's interest and concern was genuine. Then he said, "Now, the second issue is your request for approval for several hours of phone time, submitted to me by the Recreation Center officer. This request consists of several other inmates signing up for phone times and yielding these times to you. It is also your desire to use these phone times to help guide your girls' softball team in a national softball tournament in Tennessee. I acknowledge that your file consists of several letters submitted to the judge at your sentencing. I also am aware of the time and effort you spent coaching and helping these girls pursue their educational ambitions. I also have a daughter, although she is perhaps not as athletically inclined. However, this is a federal prison, and you are here of your own doing. I would like to hear from your counselor."

My counselor said, "The prison has rules about conducting business or promoting business while you are incarcerated, especially if the business is the reason you are in prison. However, this is an unusual request and it's not related to business. I have no objection to this request."

The Warden sat silent for a moment, then quickly stood up from his chair and said, "In the interest of these young girls, I will approve the request. But all prison regulations concerning phone privileges will be strictly enforced. All inmates participating in this telephone dilemma must be in good standing for phone privileges. All inmates must appear at their assigned times to yield their phone time to you. If an inmate doesn't show for his phone time at the Recreation Center officer's desk at his assigned time, his time will be vacated. Good luck with your team!"

My counselor and I swiftly left the Control Center. He informed me that food could not be taken from the kitchen and transferred to me during my phone sessions, so "conduct yourself accordingly." I thanked my counselor for his support and went back to my job. I had forgotten to secure my paintbrush; it was hard and dried out. I spent the remaining 45 minutes of the workday cleaning the paintbrush. I left my job and proceeded to the Maintenance Building to be counted and signed out. I took my happy walk to the mailroom. I pawed through my mail and went back to my bunk, where I read my letters and held back the usual sadness. My team was preparing to leave for the tournament. The truth about their softball skills was about to be tested. In 48 hours they would experience their first National Tournament game. I felt another knot in my stomach.

I went over to the gym and shot a few basketballs before supper. I joined Gabby at the chow table. He now had 43 inmates signed up for phone times on the weekend. These inmates didn't know even one of my players, and most likely never would, but they were happy doing this. It made them a part of something in the outside world, gave them a chance to do something that has a result to it. How often can an inmate participate in a situation like this and feel good about it? How often can people bond with something they haven't seen, let alone in a prison? The tempo of expectations was starting to accelerate.

We left chow and watched the inmates' team play their league game. I could sense an extra keen interest from Gabby. All of a sudden he seemed to know and connect to his daughter, without ever talking to or seeing her.

After watching the prison team win the game, we went for our walk. Gabby was going over his list of telephone sign-ups. Gabby told me that more inmates wanted to be involved. They wanted to stand by the phone sign-ups, in case some inmates were no-shows. Now I was starting to sense that a portion of this compound wanted to stake their claim of involvement. We were getting more visitors stopping by to view my team picture. Gabby was starting to act like a giddy adolescent accepting a prize he never expected. His expression was starting to brighten as Friday drew closer.

I fidgeted as I lay in bed that night. I wanted Thursday to come and go so that I could focus on Friday night.

Thursday morning came. I knew this would be a long day. I reported to my painting job. I kept busy. Time goes by fast when you're busy. That day at lunch, some of the inmates walked slowly by me and touched my shoulder and gave me the thumbs up. The rest of the workday went fast. My trip to the mailroom yielded a few letters. There were three special-looking letters from my kids. I read them first. It was sad, but their wishes for the team's success this weekend cheered me up. I pawed through the rest of the mail. I read the letters slowly. My team was leaving for Tennessee about now. The 1400 miles that separated us didn't make any difference; I felt the presence of a coach whose leadership would hang in the balance. For the next three days I'd have to take my customary place as the coach of my team with a telephone! My shoulders felt heavy as I walked to the chow hall. I found Gabby and placed my soup and Jell-O down on the table next to him. My appetite just wasn't there. Gabby tried to stimulate some interest out of me. I was tight. I wanted to walk. I wanted tomorrow.

Gabby and I went for our usual walk. It was a walk of me thinking. I could smell the cigarettes of the guys following us. People in here walked while they smoked. I'm not a smoker and I don't drink. But I'm an inmate just like the walkers and the smokers. Gabby asked me what I would do the next night. I looked at him. "Nothing I can say on a telephone is going to help these girls win their softball games."

Gabby answered, "What the hell are you talking about?"

I said, "Gabby, you want delicate, you talk to a priest. You talk to me as a friend, you get candor."

Gabby said, "That's not right," expressing his contempt.

A voice from the smokers' crowd behind us told Gabby to cool it. The smokers told Gabby, "The only bullshit is that the rest of those phone guys you promised had better show up this weekend."

I yelled, "Let's just walk."

For once, it sounded like there was another team on the compound besides the prison softball team. This time I had a different kind of team behind me. Somehow, a team of inmates had become a booster club supporting a girls' softball team that they never knew and might never know. The walk became faster and more vocal. Go All Sports! Go All Sports! Yea! Yea!

Somehow, I became important, and my softball team became important to a supporting cast of fans. Funny, we never had this many fans back in Michigan. Maybe, for a while, we all shared a moment as if we weren't in prison. We had something to look forward to, besides head count and chow time. The weekend was beginning to look a lot more interesting and exciting. We all left our walk for the bunk building; it was head count time. It was shower time. It was the night before the start of the National Tournament. It was bedtime. In a few more hours my team would be pulling into Tennessee for their bedtime.

# THE NATIONAL TOURNAMENT

The next morning, Gabby wanted to walk to breakfast with me. He discussed his plans for the inmates reporting to the phone center at 5:00 p.m. This was Friday. This was the start of National Girls' Softball Tournament. This was Gabby's day, and his fellow inmates', to make good on their promise for their phone times. As I went through the motions of my workday, I felt like I had an audience. Everywhere I went I got the thumbs up. Even some of the hacks gave their nod of approval. Suddenly, a prison camp in Duluth, Minnesota, 1400 miles from Tennessee, had an interest in a girls' softball team. The air felt energized. Somehow, the heavy shoulders I'd been experiencing lately became lighter. Out of nowhere, a supporting cast was behind me. Armed with this new energy, I bypassed the mailroom after work and went directly to my bunk area. I collected some paper and pencils and prepared myself for phone calls to Diamond #1 in Tullahoma, Tennessee.

I was ready. After the 4:00 p.m. head count, I went to chow. There was Gabby, sitting with about 16 inmates. Gabby motioned for me to join them. Gabby called out their names, and said, "This is your lineup for tonight. They're ready, coach." Holding back tears was beginning to be routine for me now. I acknowledged their support. I thanked them. I looked at everyone and said, "Let's do it!"

All of us started our walk to the phone center. The first six inmates signed in with the Recreation Center guard and forfeited the next 90 minutes to me. It was my turn. I walked to the guard's desk and signed in. At exactly 5:45 p.m. I placed my collect call to softball Diamond #1 in Tullahoma, Tennessee. One of the coaches hurriedly answered and accepted the call. The coach told me that the opening ceremonies had gone very well. He said that the girls looked nervous. He also told me that our first game was to begin in 30 minutes on Diamond #8 in an adjacent complex about 200 yards away. This told me that the phone couldn't help us for the first game. I told my coach to relax and not to appear nervous in front of the team, and that I would call him back at that phone an hour and a half later. I hung up and told Gabby and the other guys that their game was at the other end of the complex and that I would call them back at 7:30 p.m. I also told the guard. So, we let some of the inmates make their calls while the 90 minutes passed. Finally, it was 7:30 p.m. Again, the knot in my stomach appeared. My coach accepted the collect call. His first words: "I'm sorry, we lost to Washington." He told me that the team looked flat and played nervous. "Like not to lose, instead of playing to win. They played in a lackluster way at times. Maybe the long drive. We have no excuses. We lost." I told the coach, "It ain't over 'til it's over. Get the team back to the hotel and assemble them in the conference room at 8:30. I'll call then – put me on the speaker phone."

I hung up, walked slowly back to Gabby and the other guys. They could see it on my face. I said, "7 – 4, we lost. There's plenty of softball left."

I told the guard I was calling again at 8:30 p.m. The phones times were available to other inmates again for another hour. I walked out of the Recreation Center with a bunch of heads-down inmates. It was quiet. I wanted to think and walk. I felt I owed an explanation to these guys and to Gabby. I told everyone with us that it was only one loss in a two-game elimination tournament. "We'll do it the hard way."

I knew it would take eight straight wins now to win it. My shoulders became heavy and my walk was slower. I thought: "What do I tell these young girls when I call them in about 45 minutes?" I searched for the right choice of words. The last 21 months of my life flashed through me. I remembered my old saying: "Fame or success is a great test of character. Do you find or lose yourself as a result of it? There comes a time to erase failures and claim success."

I needed unflagging optimism. Our walk directed us back to the Phone Center. Confidently I walked to the guard desk and proceeded to my 8:30 phone call. My coach sadly accepted my collect call. Without hesitation, I said to my coach, "Please call 911. Our team is missing. They were supposed to be in Tennessee for the National Tournament. Where are they?"

Two weak voices spoke out. "We're sorry." I yelled back, "You're sorry! Tell me what you're sorry for! Are you sorry that you didn't have enough time to write postcards to your boyfriends, telling them how big the Great Smokey Mountains are? Are you sorry you couldn't make enough phone calls to your friends? Are you sorry you ran out of film taking pictures of each other? Are you sorry you didn't take the time to focus on your game? Did you know you had a softball game to play this evening?

The only phone calls of record should be to your parents, telling them you have arrived safely, and giving them the hotel phone number and your room number. Don't tell me you're sorry. Tell your teammates you're sorry. You guys let each other down. What's really sorry about all this is that you're a much better team than what showed up tonight. You know what, team? There is an antidote for all this. You guys left an unforgettable impact on girls' softball back in Michigan. Most important of all, together you players connected with something larger than wins or losses: your faith and loyalty to each other. It's not too late. It's time to ante up and honor each other. It's time to be heroes to each other! I don't have too many proud moments being in here, but I do have one proud moment every night. Before I climb into bed, I look up at your team picture. I will keep on looking at your team picture every night until I leave here. This moment no one can take away from me. Now, I want to talk to the coaches alone."

I heard the team leave the conference room. Then I said, "Coaches, are you hearing me?" They replied that they were. I said, "It's time to only think positive and act with confidence. It's going to be a long weekend. Keep the girls off their feet as much as possible. You're going to have to play and win eight straight to win it all. Tired feet mean slow running and slow reactions. Whenever you win the toss for home team before the game, bat first and try to rack up runs. There is a mercy rule of 10 runs after five innings of play. We need short games and time off the girls' feet. When you have a good lead in a game, rest your starters, but make sure you go for the wins first.
"

The coaches told me that they were going to play on Saturday at 9 a.m., 12 p.m., 3 p.m., 6 p.m. and 8 p.m. – if they kept winning. We agreed to the phone calls about an hour after each game. I said, "I'm not going to wish them good luck. They don't need luck. Just play hard. The results will be there. Get the rest. Good night." I hung up.

I walked past the Recreation guard. Everyone was gone except for Gabby and about 16 of our inmate followers. I told Gabby, "Don't count this team out. It's going to get very interesting this weekend." Gabby said a lot of people heard the tempo of my phone conversation. Everyone was listening, even the guards. We walked back to our bunk area. I stared at the team picture and looked at Gabby with a grin. I said, "You know, the girls on this team don't really know how good they are!" With that thought, I allowed myself to indulge in a good night's sleep. I felt good and I knew Gabby was ready with his brigade of inmates ready to share their phone times for the long weekend ahead.

It was a 6:30 a.m. wake-up for me on Saturday morning. I rushed through a shower and showed up at breakfast to a friendly greeting from Gabby and 27 inmates. We talked about the phone times. The attitude and spirit of everyone armed us with new energy. Somehow, we forgot about prison. For a while, we were a part of something beyond the compound that dictated our life here.

We had a little time before the phone calls, so we walked the compound for a short time, then went to the Phone Center. It was 8:30 and the first 12 inmates signed in for their phone times and forfeited their times over to me. Our first game was at 9:00. My first call to one of the coaches was at 9:30. I wanted an update on the game. Our game was on Diamond #7 at the west end of the softball complex. It was about a three-minute walk to the concession stand near Diamond #1. The collect call was accepted by my coach. His first words were, "We're winning 6-0." We agreed to a 10:15 a.m. call. I hung up and walked over to my followers and looked at Gabby.

"6-0, we're winning, 5$^{th}$ inning." Smiles appeared on everyone. Even the hacks showed an acknowledgement. I walked over to the coffee machine, inserted a token, and started sipping my coffee. I now had the chance to let the scheduled inmates makes their phone calls for the next two time slots. Gabby and I were relaxed. No team had ever come back to beat us with a 6-run lead.

It was 10:15 – a collect call to my coach. We won, 7-1. We beat a team from Kansas. I kept repeating myself to the coach, "Keep the girls off their feet." "Good job!"

We had a 12 p.m. game. We agreed on a 1 p.m. update call on the game. Again, there was time to allow some inmates for their phone calls. We had about a two-hour wait. The schedule allowed us to have lunch at 11:30. I wasn't hungry, but it was something to do. About 17 of us took our walk around the compound after lunch. We were back at the phone center at 12:15. The #7 slot at the phone area was vacant. I signed in and placed my collect call. A happy response – we were winning, 4-1. I said, "Hang up and get back to the team."

I walked back to our group and told them, "We're winning 4-1 against a team from Wisconsin." Some of the inmates took their turns at the phones. When it was about 1:45, I decided to place my call. We beat Wisconsin 5-2 and our next game was at 3 p.m. against a team from Tennessee.

We left the phones open for inmates until 3:30 p.m. We stayed in the phone center and drank soda. I told Gabby, "I hope we don't play a team that's local in Tennessee, because we may not get the close call from the umpires."

My 3:30 phone call revealed that we were in a scoreless game after four innings. My serious-looking walk back to my gang brought a simple answer: "No score after four innings." The tone of our area of the phone center was low-key and quiet.

At about 4:30 I looked at Gabby and said, "I think they're waiting for my call." I placed the call. We won, 2-0. Before I hung up, I looked toward the group with a thumbs-up sign. I asked my coach to make sure they got take-out food for the players so the girls could rest. Our next game was at 6 p.m. against a team from Alabama. We agreed on a 6:30 p.m. update call.

Gabby and I left the phone center. Some of the inmates stayed on to make their phone calls. I went back to my barracks and took a bed rest before supper. Gabby came by and we walked to the chow hall. Gabby asked me if I was nervous. I said I wasn't, but I was concerned about the stamina of these girls, playing 5 games in 11 hours. But I really believed they were mentally prepared and they knew where the finish line was. Gabby and I had a slow supper and we arrived at the phone center at 6 p.m. There was a new guard at the desk. It was female guard and she was aware of the situation. We now had formed an alliance of about 45 inmates looking on. I signed in for my 6:30 call. The line was busy on the other end. I was mute. How could this be? I kept trying and the operator kept saying "Sorry, it's still busy." I sat in phone area #7 with a busy signal until about 7:15 p.m. My call was finally accepted. My coach said that a woman in the concession stand had been using the phone in her office. The coach told the woman that this was a private phone stationed in the concession stand for our use. After checking with her manager, she apologized. We had won, 10-2 against the team from Alabama. I displayed the thumbs-up to Gabby. There were some cheers. I didn't have the time to talk too long. We had an 8 o'clock game against a team from Nebraska, and it was 7:30. We hung up. I walked over to a happy crowd. I said, "Four down and four to go." We all stayed at the phone center. No one left. It was getting interesting! There was continuing upbeat behavior from our followers and a few more were beginning to register their interest. For a lot of these inmates, it was therapeutic. They were a part of something.

I made my 8:45 update call. My coach answered, "Mercy rule: we won, 13-1. Game's over." Again the thumbs-up to the group. The Phone Center shut down at 9:15; I wanted to discuss the next day's schedule and how the team was holding together. My coach told me that they were tired. I told him to keep them off their feet, get them some food and tell them to soak in the tub; it would be good for their muscles. My coach told me, "We have been playing 12 to 14 girls. Everyone's firing on all pistons. We have a 10 a.m. game with a team from Ohio. Should we win – and we will – we will have to beat a team from Florida twice, because they are undefeated." I told the coach to tell the team I was proud of them, and I'm going to give their team picture by my bedside an extra smile of a proud and confident coach.

Gabby was waiting for me. We had to hurry back to our bunk area for the Saturday night head count at 9:30.

That night I couldn't sleep. Our next games would be on Diamond #1, where the phone was. My coach told me he couldn't wait to play on Diamond #1. They needed my help. They were now in an area of a somewhat paralyzing feeling. Our basic skills needed to come into play here, with the ending writing itself. I was to make an 8:30 call to the team in the conference room of the hotel.

I woke up Sunday morning at 6:40. I showered and went to breakfast. At 7:30 I went for a walk. I needed to be alone. This was a walk to prepare myself for a phone conversation to the softball team poised to take the next step to set the stage for a national championship game. It was time for me to ante up. I had created the environment that brought this team together. Now, it was my turn. My weapons would be a telephone and the emotional attachment with my team that 1400 miles couldn't separate. At 10 this morning, I had to be on Diamond #1 in Tullahoma, Tennessee, traveling by telephone. This was my road map. I walked over to the Phone Center. Gabby was there with about 18 other inmates. They knew I was serious. I had no smiles for my loyal followers. This morning I had to be a coach. I needed to leave everything else aside. I place the collect phone call to my team in the conference room at the hotel. I was on speaker phone. I wasted no time.

"Hello, team and good morning!" The team was loud with their response: "Hi coach, we're ready!" I said, "Team, I want you to know I'm proud of you. You did not quit and you fought back like real winners!" I said, "Today is about who you are. Today is a day you will remember for the rest of your lives. Together, we will finish what we started 16 months ago. We will together witness the results of your visions. There cannot be time to feel tired. Today is the day your energy and spirit from each other will carry you through the next three games. This will write the ending of this National Tournament. Go finish the job. Meet me on Diamond #1!" I hung up the phone.

I walked back to a silent crowd of Gabby and about 30 followers. Gabby asked me if was mad at anyone. I told Gabby that "this is the way I coach. I engage my self in a very serious mood."

I had about a half hour before I placed my phone call to Diamond #1. One of my coaches would be ready with a little scouting report on this team we were playing. I wanted to discuss our game strategy before the game started. I remained in the Phone Center until about 9:45. Gabby walked over a coffee for me. It was time. I placed my call and the coach answered with the report that the team we were playing was loaded with long ball hitters.

However, they were slow runners and played a fair defensive softball game. I told the coach to "take your ups (bat first). Let's try to jump on this team early and break their spirit. We are a very fast running team and we are aggressive on defense. We always put the ball in play a lot." Our team won the coin toss, so we batted first. We jumped out front 2-0 in the first inning. We managed three more runs in the next four innings while allowing two runs. We ended up winning, 5-2.

I was on the phone for 78 minutes. I needed a break. The next game was at 1 p.m., against the undefeated Florida team. We had to beat them twice to win it. Gabby and about 24 of us went to lunch. We discussed time slots and made sure all the right inmates were ready to sign off on their phone times. I now needed about three straight hours on the phone. We all were sort of quiet. The pressure was sinking in. We were all feeling serious. I wasn't hungry. I knew that there was one thing Gabby wanted to ask me, but he knew better. He didn't want to upset my game plan by asking if his daughter was playing. This time we didn't walk. We stayed in the lunch building. We were relaxed. We just felt good. Something important was going to happen. Something was coming to a head. Somehow, we were all a part of it. Who cares if we were in prison? We forgot about prison. We had something to look forward to!

Finally it was time. All 30 of us walked to the phone center. Everyone looked at me. I looked at Gabby and said, "Relax. It's going to be fun." My stomach told me different. I made the phone call. My coach told me that the Florida team was well-stocked with good hitters and they were well-coached. He said they looked rested. I said, "Forget them. Is our team ready?" My coach didn't have to answer that. I heard the yelling and cheering of our players. The fans, the players – it became very noisy.

The electricity was there. This was what it's all about. Here we go!

We lost the coin toss and batted first. The first three innings didn't produce any runs by either team. The top of the fourth inning saw us score one run on two base hits and an error. Florida came back to score two runs. We were behind one run in the top of the sixth inning. We sent six batters to the plate, which produced three runs. We had a two-run lead, with Florida batting in the bottom of the seventh inning. We needed three outs. Florida's first batter grounded out and their second batter hit a double. Florida had a runner on second base with one out. I yelled on the phone to my coach, "Tell the team to forget that runner. Get the batter out!"

Florida's next batter flied out to center field. The runner on second tagged up and waltzed into third base. There were now two outs. I told my coach, "Place the outfielders fairly deep. We don't want nothing going over our heads for extra bases. We want the ball to stay in front of us." Our pitcher walked the next batter. This was no good. Florida had runners on third and first with two outs. I told my coach, "Call time out and go relax the team. One out is all we need." The next Florida batter hit a hard grounder to our shortstop, who then tossed the ball to second base for the force out. We won. Game over. One more to go!

I hung up and went directly for some water. I gave the thumbs up. We won, 4-2. One more to go!! We had about a 20-minute break before the championship game. I just sat there and drank water. I still had that serious look. Gabby came over and said that all the correct inmates were there for the phone sign-ins. "It's your phone." I looked up. The Recreation Center was filled with inmates.

Everyone wanted to be a part of this. I took a walk to the bathroom. I rinsed my face with cold water and patted my eyes with a wet paper towel. The Recreation Center was quiet. The phone guard appeared to be not interested in all this, but gave me that look of OK! Gabby had a bottle of water for me as I walked over to claim phone #7 for the last time. I placed the collect call to the coach about 10 minutes before game time. I said, "Coach, enjoy the ride! If we win the coin toss, take our outs. We want to bat last against this team. We must get their lead-off hitter out every inning. We need to keep the momentum from them."

I heard yelling and singing from our players. They were ready. We won the coin toss. We elected to be home team and bat last. Florida sent four batters up in the first inning. One base hit followed by three outs. The game was scoreless until the fourth inning. We scored a run on two base hits and a walk. We were leading 1-0 going into the top of the fifth inning. Florida tied the game with two hits and an error. We were all tied up in the seventh inning, 1-1. We managed to keep Florida off the bases in the top of the seventh inning. Now, it was our turn to bat in the bottom of the seventh inning, tied 1-1. Our first batter hit a double to right center. We now had one out with a runner on second. I told my coach to put in a pinch hitter for our next batter. I said, "Tell the pinch hitter to lift the ball high to the right side of the outfield." We needed our runner on second base to get to third base. The execution worked; our batter moved our second base runner to third base by hitting a fly ball to right field. We now had two outs and our runner was now at third base and our lead-off hitter – who was like a jack rabbit, with fast legs – was up. I told the coach to call a time out. I said to my coach, "Listen carefully. Tell our lead-off hitter to hit the second good pitch slowly on the ground to the shortstop and don't look back while running to first base. They'll never throw our hitter out – she's too fast." I also said, "Make sure our runner on third base knows what's going on. Tell the runner on third to break for home plate fast and slide into home." I said, "Look, coach, if it doesn't work, the game is still tied. We go into extra innings." My coach left the phone. About two minutes went by. Then I heard, "Run! Run! Run!" Then all of a sudden the roar of yelling and cheering. I hung up the phone. I have heard those cheers too many times in the past to wonder what happened. We won!

I walked away from the phone with that triumphant grin and a smile that held the tears on my cheeks. Gabby muttered, "Holy shit, they won." Gabby followed me out of the Recreation Center. We shared a guarded moment. 40, 50, 60 – hell, I don't know how many inmates followed us, chanting All Sports! All Sports! All Sports!

Gabby said, "Why did you hang up the phone?" I answered, "Gabby, it's their celebration. Let them have their moment." I was happy! For today I was their coach again. While I was walking, in my mind I could still hear my team cheering and yelling. My walk was proud and swift. I looked at Gabby and said, "You know Gabby, no one is there asking my players, 'You're National Champions! What are you going to do next? Are you going to Disney World?'" I said, "Their picture won't be on bubble gum cards."

For a moment I was in Tullahoma, Tennessee. By now, there had to be about 100 inmates walking with us. I wasn't tired. I wanted to walk. I was frozen in the moment. It was a cleansing feeling. I felt no weight on my shoulders. The sad days were erased. My ears kept repeating that spirit of jubilation that rang out on the phone. My players were being forged together for a lifetime of memories by a bat, a ball and a Sunday afternoon in a small town in Tennessee. I told Gabby I wanted to thank the inmates for their interest and the sacrifice of their phone times. Gabby stopped the walk and yelled, "Shut up for a moment! Mr. Short-Time Coach has something to say." I looked at all the guys and yelled out, "Even though this is not the customary place, on behalf of my girls' softball team and myself, our grateful thanks to all of you." We walked and we walked. Some of the inmates following us tapered off. It was time for supper. We went to the chow hall. I ate like a pig. I asked Gabby to stop by our bunk area that night before head count. "I have something to tell you," I said.

Gabby and I for a while found a temporary sanctuary from the prison routine. Gabby came by my bunk area that night. He had a puzzled look on his face and asked, "What's up, Short Time?" I smiled at Gabby and walked him through that last inning of our championship game. I told Gabby that I had installed a pinch hitter with our runner on second base and that she had hit a deep fly ball to the right side of the outfield. The ball was caught, but it allowed our second base runner to advance to third base. This runner had eventually scored the winning run. I then looked Gabby straight in the eyes and said, "The pinch hitter was your daughter."

Gabby paused and tried to hold back a tear. Then he said, "Unbelievable." I think Gabby wanted to show an appreciative hug, but it's against the rules to hug inmates. I said, "Gabby, if you want to ask questions about your daughter's involvement with this team, there's plenty of time left to answer your questions."

That night I spent a couple of hours writing a letter to my coaches and the team. I wanted them to know how proud I was of them and that they gave me new energy and self-acceptance to combat the remainder of my time here. I was mentally tired and gave a happy grin to my team's picture as I enjoyed a good night's sleep.

# THE CLINIC

The next couple of days I kept busy with my painting job and preparing for the Warden's Saturday softball clinic. The Warden and the hacks had been fair to me. It was my turn to give them a first-class clinic. The Recreation Center guard summoned me from my painting to his office. The guard told me that all of the equipment I requested for the clinic would be at the softball field on Saturday at 10 a.m. The guard also said, "That must be some girls' softball team you have back home." I replied, "Yes, and thank you."

My mailbox was filled with more letters from players, parents and newspaper articles about our National Championship. What a rewarding experience!

I sometimes sensed a feeling of hostility from the other inmates. Maybe I was being too much of a figure with the hacks. There was silent, resentful behavior from some inmates. I didn't care; it wouldn't be long before I took that cab ride out of here. I was a little concerned for

Gabby, because he still had a couple of years before release.

That Friday before the clinic, Gabby and three other inmates and I discussed the game plan for the clinic. The five of us would attempt to teach, show, and offer advice to some 200 inmates about the game of softball. For most inmates, this would be entertainment. To others, it could be important and informational. The five of us agreed to meet for breakfast at 7:30 on Saturday. I wanted to arrive at the softball field an hour before the clinic began, to set the bases out and chalk the base lines.

We walked over to the softball field to find a prison truck unloading bats, softballs, and a portable P.A. system. We set everything up and chalked the base lines. It was about 15 minutes before the start of the clinic when they started coming in, in pairs and foursomes. The inmates filled both sides of the bleachers. About four prison station wagons approached with kids – girls and boys. We were told they were the hacks' kids. Those kids were placed in the outer infield, by shortstop. The lieutenant with the microphone in hand welcomed everyone to the Warden-sponsored softball clinic. The lieutenant introduced me after telling everyone about my coaching background and of course my team's recent National Championship.

I proceeded with the clinic, teaching the correct way to run bases, hit, field and showing appropriate stretching exercises to be used before and after softball practices and games. I then offered a question and answer period. I was met with questions from inmates speaking broken English and those with biceps that filled out their short-sleeve shirts. Some of these inmates really didn't care; it was something to do. Some inmates seemed to attack my knowledge of softball. The clinic lasted about two hours before another prison truck pulled up with barrels of ice filled with soda pop. The prison had the grounds maintenance department clean up and load the equipment into trucks.

I spent the remainder of the day walking and reading mail. Sunday morning I made it to Mass. The church was filled with about 80 inmates.

The next three months were the same-old-same-old. Four head counts, three meals, mail reading and looking at that same old poster in the chow hall about choking. I devoted a lot of time to the prison library. I was writing a short book for student athletes seeking college athletic scholarships. It was about 90 pages of "Dos and Don'ts" about contacting college coaches to pursue a softball or baseball scholarship. I was able to secure help from a couple of teachers doing time for tax evasion. Gabby and I still walked together on the days when it wasn't too cold.

On December 1, we had a blizzard. You could not see five feet in front of you. The hacks assembled a yellow and black rope from our building to the chow hall. Holding the rope, we walked with one hand on the back of the person who was in front of us. What an experience! It was scary.

# BACK HOME

On December 5, three days prior to my release, I was instructed to make contact with each department head in the compound. Each department head hack had to sign a release form verifying, for example, that I had no books due to the prison library, or the clothing department releasing me of any extra outstanding shoes or clothes due to the department.

My softball team had sent me a team picture after the championship game. I shared the picture with Gabby and asked Gabby to sign the back of the picture. Gabby and I made the rounds to the other inmates who gave up their phone times for me during the tournament.

The night of December 7 finally came. This was to be my last night at the Federal Prison in Duluth. Gabby and a few other inmates and I made my final walk around the compound. We shared the softball team memories. You're not supposed to make friends in this place, but I couldn't help feeling that Gabby and I shared a common bond. And to me, this was an unforgettable cast of characters. It was time to take our last walk together to the barracks. Gabby walked me back to my bunk area. I took my team picture from the wall and gave it to Gabby. I told Gabby that I would not tell his daughter that her father was my friend in here. We both agreed that at another time he would tell his daughter, at another time away from this place.

That night I stayed awake most of the night. My mind and my shoulders once more felt heavy. The next part of my life stood before me. And tomorrow belonged to me. This had been an experience. People say different things about prison life. Yes, it sucks! But you make your stay in a prison by the way you accept it. If you understand why you're here and try to fabricate yourself into a well-behaved inmate, you will (hopefully) become an obedient citizen in your quest for acceptance. Some become casualties of the overcrowded compounds of concrete called penitentiaries. Others become a number isolated from the community. There are no psychiatrists listening for $100/hour to aid us back into society. You must learn to make small beginnings.

I think I slept about three hours before Gabby looked into my bunk area to join me for breakfast. It was 6:30 a.m. We walked over to the chow hall. This was my last time to read that some old *choking* poster on the wall. This was my last breakfast with a friend who made my stay a little easier. We walked back to our bunk area. Gabby wanted to show me his bedside. There on the wall was my team's picture. It was now Gabby's turn to smile at the picture. I think he was closer to his daughter, somehow. I think Gabby had found something he became a part of.

The hack came looking for me. He didn't call me inmate #D-65-0295. He said, "Well, Coach, get your gear together and report to the Control Center in 30 minutes. Your time is up."

I hustled up my gear in a duffle bag supplied by the prison. A couple of other inmates came by to say "Good luck." I looked at Gabby and said, "Thanks for being a friend. Go home to your family; our team could use another fan."

I walked away toward the Control Center. When I arrived, I surrendered my prison clothes. I was 35 pounds lighter and my street clothes were loose on me. A doctor gave me a physical. The discharge lieutenant gave me the personal belongings that I had checked in with. The lieutenant gave me a voucher for a bus ticket out of Duluth, to St. Paul, to Chicago, to Detroit. He also gave me $60 in cash and a signed softball from my softball team. He told me that the ball had been sent to me back in October, but it had to remain with my discharge belongings. The guard also gave me instructions to report directly to the halfway house upon arriving in Detroit. Then they instructed me to wait in the lobby. I waited in the lobby until 11:48 a.m., the exact time that I had come in the previous May. The lieutenant once again came out to inform me that the taxi was here to take me to the bus depot in downtown Duluth. He also told me that the cab ride was prepaid and that the driver was not allowed to stop for me to talk to anyone. That sounded puzzling to me. The lieutenant wished me good luck and I entered the cab, with $60 to my name. As we slowly started to leave the compound, I looked back for one last look.

As we approached the front gate, I noticed some commotion. As we moved closer, I saw that two hack trucks were stationed near the entrance gate. We slowly proceeded through the gate – an unbelievable sight! On both sides of the road, my softball team was lined up. It was an assembly line of players in uniform, some fans, and a pick-up truck with a six-foot trophy. It was the National Championship trophy. The cab driver looked back at me, and said, "I can't stop, but I can drive very slowly." Yellow roses were thrown at the cab with cheers and chants: "Coach! Coach!" The cab driver opened his window and caught as many roses as he could and handed them back to me. We almost came to a complete stop. I looked back – the yelling continued. The cab driver noticed the tears on my face. I was mute, and the knot in my stomach tightened.

It had been a long time since I'd seen my players. We had all learned that sometimes you have to get knocked down to know how to get up.

The 1978 All Sports team persevered and accomplished what many thought was impossible. They won the Softball National Championship.

In 1980 the team went on to win their second National Softball Championship. The team proudly surrounds their hard earned trophy.

# **Tributes**

Softball may have been the game; but there was more to learn than the rules. In order to play for Coach Bud, you needed to have perseverance and real dedication.

I was one of the lucky ones to have had the chance to play for a coach who had such a deep dedication to the teaching of the sport. We not only developed as players but as individuals. The team goal was not only to win but also to execute precisely. Our practices were long, repetitive and exhausting.

Even though Coach Bud was tough on us while on the field, his caring for each of us didn't stop after we left the ballpark. He had a knack for finding talent and he knew just how far he could push us. Coach Bud saw something in me as well as in many of my teammates and went out of his way to provide us with opportunities that we would not have gotten on our own. Coach Bud had a real desire to promote his players and was very instrumental in helping many of us receive athletic scholarships to major universities.

My most memorable experience playing for Coach Bud, was what happened after a league game. We came away with the win; but our level of play didn't meet the coach's expectations. As we shook hands with our opponent and proceeded to put our equipment away, the team was ordered to get back on the field. The spectators were stunned and couldn't believe that our coach called a practice upon securing a victory. The practice continued for several hours and we thought it would never end. Therefore, the team came up with a plan to end the practice. Coach Bud always pitched batting practice, so we made it everyone's goal to hit the coach. Odds were bet on Laurie and me as the favorites since we were known for line drives up the middle. As far as we knew, Coach Bud had no knowledge of our scheme. One by one, we took our turns and I become the victorious one. I hit a line shot up the middle off the shin of our coach and practice was finally called.

We enjoyed the grueling practices because Coach Bud was able to convince us that this was the only way to become Champions. And by Champions, I don't just mean winning games. However, we did win our fair share of championships along the way. Coach Bud taught each of us to believe in ourselves so that we not only succeeded on the field; but in our lives as we all have grown into adults. The courage to believe in yourself and the friendships that we developed created a foundation that I hope everyone gets to experience. I feel that I have accomplished many great things in my life from making All Star Teams, winning National Championships, receiving an athletic scholarship, getting a collegiate education, having a career to being a wife and mother. I believe it all stems from having met people like Coach Bud.

As I watch some of the great movies produced today like "Remember the Titans" and The Miracle, memories of playing softball for a great coach runs through my mind.
-   *Mary, Center Fielder*

I was one of the coaches for Coach Bud's girls' softball team. I have been involved in sports all of my life, and have seen a lot of coaches in different sports. Coach Bud was the complete package. He was the toughest and most disciplined coach I have ever experienced. He was motivating and none of his players ever challenged his thinking or his strategy.

In the final analysis, it goes far beyond that. There were personalities and feelings to deal with.

Was Coach Bud a softball fanatic? No, it was merely pride in the results. Two National Championships and several second-place finishes. Seventeen of his players were awarded college softball scholarships.

This is a mere record of the past, but what it conveyed cannot be forgotten. Coach Bud's only mistake was that he devoted all of his time, energy and money to everyone else.

Coach Bud's softball seasons have ended. The memory of them takes a place alongside those of yesteryear and will become topics of future conversations.

A player on a women's softball team told me that every softball player should play for Coach Bud, once in her lifetime.

-   *Coach Al*


I was an avid fan of Bud Hucul's girls softball team! My family and I experienced mouch enjoyment and were amazed at the ability and discipline of the girls playing softball.

They were the team!

-   *S. W. Pierce*

Coach Bud Hucul was a pioneer of USSA Youth and Women's Softball. He hosted one of the most successful women's USSA World Tournaments in Michigan in 1974.

His background in baseball and softball impacted much of his knowledge to his players. Coach Bud was very successful in coaching girl's and women's softball.

As players, we practiced hard, learned a lot, and had fun traveling all over the country.

- *Linda Mueller, Second-base. Member of the USSA Softball Hall of Fame*

# EPILOGUE

Upon Coach Bud's release from Federal prison, he continued to coach his girls' softball team. The following year, Coach Bud's team finished 3rd in the National Softball Tournament. The next year they won the National Championship again.

In the three-year period that his team played in the National Championship Tournament, Coach Bud saw 17 of his players receive college softball scholarships. His career was mostly about little people making a stand for themselves. After coaching girls' softball for 21 years, Coach Bud retired with two National Softball Championships, four second-place finishes and one third-place finishes to his credit.

Coach Bud's teams shared in a record of 1,246 wins while losing only 244. He helped level the playing field for many young girls playing softball.

Coach Bud's goal is to operate a safe shelter, which would provide health care, education and recreational activities for runaway and abused girls.

*There is speculation that Coach Bud was recruited by the FBI.*

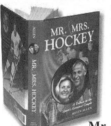

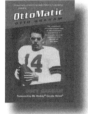

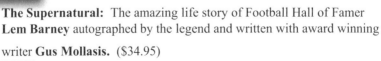

# A MESSAGE FROM THE PUBLISHER

We are very proud to present the extraordinary story of the legendary 1978 National Championship Softball Team, All Sports. The book *22 Yellow Roses* by *Clarence Hucul* has been artfully crafted and this remarkable story of a coach's dream to bring his team to a National Championship at any cost deserves to be immortalized. We are truly grateful to *Clarence Hucul* for sharing this memorable event with all of us. Immortal Investments Publishing is honored to present *22 Yellow Roses*. It will inspire readers now and in future generations!

*Michael J. Reddy*
*Publisher*

Immortal Investments Publishing produces timeless books that move, inspire, and spotlight the best of the human spirit manifested by extraordinary human achievement.

Please review and order our other outstanding titles by visiting www.immortalinvestments.com or by calling **1-800-475-2066.**

Please let us know if you have suggestions for other exceptional books or have comments about *22 Yellow Roses*.

\*\*\*This publishing venture is revolutionary in that the book like all other Immortal Investment titles is not distributed to bookstores. It is available exclusively through Immortal Investments Publishing.

To bring *Clarence Hucul* to your event for a personal book signing and softball coach's clinic please contact www.immortalinvestments.com.

### Order your signed copy of
### 22 Yellow Roses
### by Clarence Hucul  today!
### 1-800-475-2066

## NOT SOLD IN BOOKSTORES
Immortal Investmants Publishing
35122 W. Michigan Ave. Wayne, MI 48184

# <u>boji books</u> PRESENTS...

# College-Bound
# Student-Athletes
# Seeking Athletic Scholarships

Our book offers valuable
information to student athletes.

It shows how to be heavily recruited.

Other important information included:

- ❖ When to contact colleges and how to
  write cover letters.
- ❖ Recruiting techniques by an author
  who has personally secured many
  athletic scholarships for the average,
  but talented student athlete.
- ❖ 12 chapters of valuable information
  that Middle School athletes, parents,
  and NCAA rules that the average
  students does not have access to.
- ❖ What you should say and not say in
  your application and interviews.

Immortal Investments Publishing
35122 W. Michigan Ave.
Wayne, MI 48184
www.immortalinvestments.com
## 1-800-475-2066
## $9.95 plus $4.00 S&H